Terroir

Terroir

Love, Out of Place

NATASHA SAJÉ

Trinity University Press | *San Antonio, Texas*

Trinity University Press
San Antonio, Texas 78212
Copyright © 2020 Natasha Sajé

"love is more thicker than forget," copyright © 1939, 1967, 1999 by the
Trustees for the E. E. Cummings Trust, from *E. E. Cummings: Complete
Poems, 1904–1962*, edited by George J. Firmage. Used by permission of
Liveright Publishing Corporation.

Fernando Pessoa, "To be great, be whole," from "Odes," translated by
Edwin Honig and Susan M. Brown, from *Poems of Fernando Pessoa*.
English translation copyright © 1986 by Edwin Honig and Susan M.
Brown. Reprinted with the permission of the Permissions Company on
behalf of City Lights Books.

Book design by BookMatters
Cover design by Derek Thornton, Notch Design
Cover art: Bridgeman Images 51539; Shutterstock 566962153
Author photo by David Baddley

Printed in Canada

ISBN 978-1-59534-932-3 paperback
ISBN 978-1-59534-933-0 ebook

Trinity University Press strives to produce its books using methods and
materials in an environmentally sensitive manner. We favor working
with manufacturers that practice sustainable management of all natural
resources, produce paper using recycled stock, and manage forests with
the best possible practices for people, biodiversity, and sustainability.
The press is a member of the Green Press Initiative, a nonprofit program
dedicated to supporting publishers in their efforts to reduce their
impacts on endangered forests, climate change, and forest-dependent
communities.

The paper used in this publication meets the minimum requirements of
the American National Standard for Information Sciences—Permanence
of Paper for Printed Library Materials, ANSI 39.48-1992.

CIP data on file at the Library of Congress

24   23   22   21   20   ⌒   5   4   3   2   1

Contents

Vel. Loka , li 31-7-1943 E.F.
dne

impronta del dito
Prstni odtis

IL PODESTÀ – ŽUPAN

EVEN THOUGH I HAD A GERMAN MOTHER AND WAS BORN in Munich, my identity card was inscribed "stateless," like my father's. As a captain in King Peter's Royal Yugoslav Army, he fought both Nazis and Communists, and when Britain switched allies and backed Tito, my father had to leave the country or be killed. Because of anticommunist fervor in the United States, in 1957 we received immigration visas and arrived in New York via Flying Tiger airline with two hundred dollars. I learned English from *Howdy Doody*, *Romper Room*, and in kindergarten, and by the age of eight, even though we still spoke German at home, English and its pointed syntax were colonizing my brain.

The French word *terroir* refers to the whole environment in which something—grapes, for instance—is grown: the climate, the soil, the topography. As important as the root stock and the care of grapes, the effect of terroir is less controllable and more nuanced. Perhaps, when it applies to an immigrant, terroir does more work than family to shape identity. In other words, if such factors as class, sexuality, and nationality are fluid, and family is distant, then environment becomes, metaphorically, a honey that heals wounds or a pollutant that makes it difficult to breathe. My parents' multiple dislocations shaped their views of immigration and nationality, and my own experience in an interracial marriage spurred my quest to understand racism. Working in the theocratic state of Utah sharpened my resistance to the repressive aspects of religion, particularly its persecution of gay people. The specter of class status pervades every category of identity. I have filtered these issues through the lens of place—a powerful, literally *grounding* motif. "Skies change, souls don't," wrote Horace—in error, I would argue. Whatever we are made of responds to wherever we are, and that "where" includes other people. If a neighbor had not adopted five-year-old-me as her grandchild, I would be a different person. I seek to understand how aspects of environment affect us, and although I can only speak for myself, I attempt to broaden the view by bringing in other voices.

Several summers ago I visited the coast of Croatia and three medieval seaside cities: Trogir, a stone town on its own tiny island; Zadar, with its sea organ—a modern art installation with whalelike notes that echo in my ears to this day; and Split, which was our home base. On our last evening in Split, my wife, Laura, and I were sitting on a sunny balcony of the Adriatic Club, overlooking its ancient harbor and a cove packed with boats.

I said, "We're done with this place, aren't we?" And she nodded.

That night we'd be on a car ferry to Rijeka and then on to Trieste and Venice. How did we know we were done with Split? We'd relished the traces of the Diocletian Palace, wondrously accessible under the newer city. We'd taken pleasure in the lively pedestrian squares, swimming in the sea a few steps from our apartment, and a day trip we took to the island of Brač. But we hadn't had a conversation longer than three minutes with anyone who lived in Split.

When our landlord, a scientist supplementing his income via Airbnb, came down to explain the air-conditioning, I had the unreasonable wish that he would invite us upstairs for a drink. But with so many people traipsing through, why would he? We were tourists, customers, not potential friends.

On our way to and from town, we passed an imposing new house whose mailbox displayed the name *Zvonimir Mihanović* in simple black print. Artist's paintbrushes leaned against the triangular picture window on the top floor of the white marble-clad house. The ample driveway held a black Mercedes SUV with New York license plates, a motorcycle, and a Smart car with Croatian plates. In our apartment, I looked up Zvonimir Mihanović on the internet and learned that he goes out in a boat to sketch, to have a "live encounter with his motifs," then returns to this house to paint eight to ten hours a day. Preferring a hyperrealist style, he produces just four oil paintings a year.

A live encounter with one's motifs—perhaps that applies not only to realistic visual artists but also to writers. My own motifs include language; I grew up knowing language is fickle and deceptive, and also that it shapes experience. The German word *Sehnsucht* is translated as "longing" but has deeper connotations—*Sucht* is dis-ease, an unquenchable thirst. I'm reminded that we wouldn't need language if our desires were immediately fulfilled, if we were perpetual infants with parents always present to anticipate our needs.

Perhaps my attraction to Mihanović comes from my desire to be grounded, to have a sense of home as he does. Yet philosopher Gaston Bachelard seems old-fashioned and narrowly European when he argues that childhood homes shape us forever. In the United States, capitalism-imbued restlessness—for education, jobs, and other "opportunities"—drives everyone (not just immigrants) to move households more than citizens anywhere else in the world.

I'd go back to Split if I could meet Zvonimir Mihanović. Not because he's a rich artist, or even because he's a good one, but because his creativity is drawn from the place where he was born and where he lives. His work and life, past and present, are integrated. His realist paintings have the ethereal quality of external sight revealing an internal vision. A boat in a harbor, an island coastline, disappearing rocks—his paintings are permeated with an otherworldly stillness. He paints tile roofs, the colors of coral, and dove-gray stones, turquoise or periwinkle water—always still water and always summer. "In summer, the song sings itself," wrote poet William Carlos Williams. There are no people in Mihanović's paintings, and their absence is haunting. By contrast, nineteenth-century seascapes like the early ones of Turner contain human figures, however small, to help viewers measure the natural grandeur. One doesn't so much look *at* Mihanović's paintings as *through* them to the stillness felt by the painter, a strangely intimate feeling. We are the people in his paintings. We are seeing without wave or wind, a moment of time caught between thoughts, between heartbeats, simultaneously sentient, alive, as well as lifeless, nonessential witnesses. The stillness, like realism, is an illusion. Physicist Carlo Rovelli echoes essayist Michel de Montaigne when he writes, "The entire evolution of science would suggest that the best grammar for thinking about the world is that of change, not of permanence. Not of being, but becoming." These essays explore my "becoming," and they attempt to integrate my past and present, my work and life.

Whenever Laura is asked where she is from, she proudly says, "Boston." When asked where I am from, I say, "I was born in Munich and grew up in New York." But I don't feel *from* Germany or New York or New Jersey or Indiana or Baltimore or Washington, DC, and certainly not from Salt Lake City—all places where I've lived. *From* implies more than a place; it suggests origins and authenticity. For the geographer Yi-Fu Tuan, place is security and space is freedom: "We are attached to the one and long for the other." This sounds sensible, but what if no place offers security? What if place must be worked through as though it were space and time? Like any opposition, the terms raise questions.

Determining the provenance of a painting establishes its legitimacy or reveals a theft. The provenance of a person, however, is revealed in her interactions with others, in what she makes and says and does. These interactions might pressure her to assimilate or to strengthen her differences. "Home is where the heart is" is the cliché. My heart is with those I love and in what I create. Perhaps this is true of everyone— Laura gives a simpler answer because of her connection to, and pride in, her origins.

Sixty years ago, the proportion of immigrants in the US general population comprised less than 6 percent. Even today the figure is 13.5 percent, smaller than most people think. Sometimes I feel it is crucial to distinguish myself as an outsider by rejecting the norms of the dominant order. When people learn I live in Utah, they often raise an eyebrow, and I

quickly say, "I'm not *from* Utah," hoping they'll grasp the subtext: I'm not Mormon, I moved to the state for a teaching job,
a choice, but not my first. By contrast, the United States was
my father's first choice of countries in exile. We could have
gone to Australia or to Canada, other countries that accepted
refugees in the mid-1950s.

Some peoples whose lands have been contested—the
Dalmatians, for example—know well where home is. In *Black
Lamb and Grey Falcon,* Rebecca West recounts a history that
explains the emblematic wariness of the Dalmatians: "The
conquest of Illyria by Rome, of Rome by the barbarians; then
three hundred years of conflict between Hungary and Venice;
then four hundred years of oppression by Venice with the war
against Turkey running concurrently for most of that time; a
few years of hope under France, frustrated by the decay of
Napoleon; a hundred years of muddling misgovernment by
Austria." Since West wrote that list, the Dalmatian region
has been invaded by the Nazis, incorporated into Tito's
Communist Yugoslavia, and finally, after a bitter war with
Serbia, achieved independence as Croatia in 1991. Caution
is the subtext of every encounter with outsiders; how could
Croatians be anything but watchful and vigilant?

"It is always sad to leave a place to which one knows one will
never return. Such are the melancholies du voyage: perhaps
they are one of the most rewarding things about traveling,"
wrote Gustave Flaubert, creator of Emma Bovary, a character
always seeking something other than what she has. Yet desire
is not the opposite of gratitude, and being satisfied can be
a kind of stasis, even a kind of death. In these essays, I am
returning to the past in the hope of understanding myself.

Awareness of the increasingly pressing question of how to spend my time on earth makes every choice significant.

That sense of mortality—I didn't begin to feel it until I reached my fifties. Why did it take so long? When friends were dying of AIDS, why didn't I feel that more personally? Or when my father died? Perhaps a sense of mortality is like identity itself—a process linked to living in one's own body, albeit one that moves from place to place. Perhaps prejudices, like physical frailties, have to be experienced viscerally to be truly understood. I feel temporality with diminishing eyesight, lung capacity, and muscle strength—slow erosions. In daily routines, change slips by incrementally. In returning to places by writing about them, I face loss more directly, along with regret for the ignorance of my younger self.

My first trip to the Adriatic: the town of Cattolica at age five. A professional photographer took photos of my mother, my aunt, and me, digging my wooden paddle spoon into gelato on the beach. I also remember myself sitting in the otherwise empty hotel dining room at 5 p.m., at a round table for eight with only my mother, the inn having acceded to our request for an early meal. I remember the taste and texture of the spaghetti—so unlike what my mother cooked, this chewy pasta freshly, lightly tomatoey. Outside the dining room, the beach is crowded, the town is crowded—a cheap package tour destination, although I didn't know that then. When my necklace breaks in the hotel lobby, strangers on their knees look for the beads and then place the cool glass spheres in my palm. In memory I string the beads together again as I write, a necklace that it now hurts to wear. I string together beads *of* memory, more fragile and easily scattered than those sparkling orbs of glass.

Mordwand

FROM BEHIND THE BAR, FRAU STEFFEN LOOKED ME UP and down as if appraising an animal at a livestock show. She was not quite thirty, tiny and blonde, birdlike with sharp features and large blue-gray eyes. Her nails were manicured with pink polish. Her voice suggested a hint of glass breaking.

Herr Steffen strode out of the kitchen, wiped his hands on his apron, and offered a handshake. He was flouting a European rule I'd learned: women initiate contact. In his forties, he had the florid look of a drinker.

Frau Steffen led me downstairs, below street level. I thumped my heavy suitcase on each step. When she opened the door to a room, I saw that each of the other waitresses had claimed a bed already covered with her things. Mine was in the middle, with about a foot on either side, and I banged my shin trying to get to it. The brunette waitress flicked the ashes from her cigarette into a glass ashtray on the windowsill.

The blonde waitress, whose name I remember as Suzanne, was placing her clothes into the bureau that crowded the door. After introducing us, Frau Steffen left. I wondered how to unpack without space to open my suitcase. The two women did not speak. After what felt like a long silence, I asked, "Where are you from?"

"Zurich," they said, not in unison.

"Like the Steffens," Suzanne added.

"I'm here to learn to ski," I offered. They exchanged looks. "I was working for Daimler Benz in Stuttgart, and I wanted to stay in Europe but I didn't want to au pair." Their silence made me continue. "I want to know Switzerland."

We spoke High German, a tongue almost as foreign to them as Swiss German was to me. Disdain emanated from them like the smell of cooked cabbage. They spoke to each other in rapid dialect. The brunette was younger than I but entering her fifth season of waitressing. Suzanne had worked in a grocery store before her year of waitressing.

Like me, they'd found the job through seasonal employee want ads in the fall of 1977. My Swiss friend Ursula had sent me the booklet when I told her I wanted to continue working in Europe. She suggested the village of Grindelwald, located twenty miles from where she lived in Thun, six minutes from the train station. To inject uncertainty into her life as a biology teacher, Ursula left her apartment exactly six minutes before her train. That way, if something delayed her, say a conversation with a friend, she missed the train. This, she said, made her feel that her life was unpredictable. There would, of course, soon be another train. I liked the wry way she told me this, as though describing a stranger's idiosyncrasy.

My own life felt unpredictable enough—every day I encountered a situation that baffled me, an idea that made me revise my own. In Stuttgart one of my coworkers had been a Vietnamese woman who met her German husband while he was motorcycling through Asia. She was afraid to have children because they'd be mixed-race. "I wouldn't mind a girl. But what if it's a boy?" she said. In the United States, I told her, many people are mixed-race. "But we live in Stuttgart," she replied.

The Eigerblick had offered one hundred francs a month more than the other hotel in Grindelwald—eighteen hundred francs—eight times as much as a Roman countess offered for an au pair position. I'd heard stories of au pairs being exploited, and I never liked babysitting, so it was easy to choose. Luxury restaurants and hotels still employed exclusively male servers. The Eigerblick had only three stars, but saving even my Eigerblick salary would enable me to travel for many months and then pay my way back to the United States.

Managing their last hotel in Ticino had left the Steffens with debts, the waitresses told me. Whether this was due to mismanagement or bad fortune or the condition of being German Swiss in an Italian canton—territorial allegiances replace class snobbery in Switzerland—or some combination, I never knew. But a dark cloud of debt enveloped them, and everyone who worked at the Eigerblick, all winter.

That first night my coworkers' sounds and scents kept me awake in misery. I was an only child who had never had to share a room except for a memorably awful first year in college. My college roommate had written "nonsmoker" on her housing preference form when in fact she was only *trying* to quit. The stuffy Swiss hotel room, with its three beds with white sheets so close together, smaller than my freshman dorm room, reminded me of an old photo: a row of shrouds inside caskets after the Triangle Shirtwaist factory fire in

New York City in 1911. At least our window, with a view of the loading area, was not barred.

The next day, after learning how to use and clean the coffee machine, how to write up orders, what to serve hotel guests for breakfast (bread, jam, cheese, and muesli), I walked toward the village. Not far down the road, I saw a sign, *Zimmer Frei,* and my heart took a little skip of hope.

Frau Jaun was grateful to have a steady renter and pleased to succor the American mistreated by the outsiders from Zurich. She expressed her outrage, *Ein kleines Zimmer für drei Frauen! Zwei-hundert Franken pro Monat!* She'd eaten cookies produced by Ursula's family factory, which she declared *ausgezeichnet* (outstanding). Her son studied in North Carolina. She offered me a cozy, pine-paneled corner room with a private bath directly across the hall. It cost less than the shared room at the Eigerblick.

Frau Steffen's large eyes narrowed in anger when she registered the fact that she would be getting two hundred francs less a month. I felt a twinge of fear like the moment after touching a hot stove, before the pain sets in.

The first week, I confused orders or was slow in taking them. I ruined coffees by not tamping properly or by oversteaming milk, and I screeched when I made a mess at the machine. Suzanne helped me clean it up while the other waitress smirked. After breakfast service, Frau Steffen told me to come see her at the front desk. She leaned over the account book with an elegant index finger pressed to her nose. The entry smelled of disinfectant and her floral, woody perfume.

"We didn't know you would be so clumsy."

"I'm getting better," I said, embarrassed that I had to defend myself, standing in front of the high desk like a schoolgirl.

"I can't use you for the busy evening shift, and thus, you are not worth the full salary." She shook her head and returned to her bookkeeping as if the matter were closed. She knew I'd never waitressed, so I saw this as retaliation for my moving out. My stomach churned. My brain sped through my options until I remembered an ad for an association of hotel employees in the booklet Ursula had sent.

On my first day off, pumped up with adrenaline and righteousness, I took the train to Bern to meet the association's lawyer. How did I manage this? I'm amazed at the initiative of my twenty-two-year-old self. This was the woman who in college never spoke in class. Who accepted an erroneous grade rather than confront the professor. Who, heart pounding, stood outside a party she'd been invited to, unable to knock on the door. Who returned to her dorm room, defeated.

Matter-of-factly, the lawyer said, "The Steffens may not reduce your pay as you have not misrepresented your lack of experience. A contract is a contract." He sent them a letter, which in efficient Switzerland arrived the next morning.

After this, even Herr Steffen, who had been more jovial toward me than his wife, tried to be stern and silent. He avoided his usual talk about the junk Americans eat and the huge cars they drive. About silly Jimmy Carter and his peanuts. My coworkers looked at me with—what? Not respect, not envy, and not gratitude for making more space in the bedroom. Instead, they looked through me, as if I were glass. I responded with determination—if I screwed up the coffee machine, I meticulously, silently, repaired the damage. I would show them what I was made of.

Each evening I returned to my room with its red gingham curtains and yellow cotton-covered down comforter in a chalet that smelled like stone and pine and the summer hay piled up in the barn to feed the cows in winter. Some people feel comfort from knowing exactly where they are in relation to the landscape, as one does in a mountain valley. But without a horizon, a limitless view at which to gaze, one can also feel claustrophobic. At night, I could be Heidi, snug in her comfortable loft. But each morning I pulled on my snow boots and trudged up the hill to the hotel, closed in by the mountain range. I was Cinderella without hope of a prince.

The list of my year and a half of romantic experiences in Europe was brief: bad sex with a casino employee on the ship from New York to Cherbourg; bad sex with a friend from college; a crush on my boss in Paris; a crush on a woman in my writing group; getting picked up by the son of a Turkish diplomat, a blue-eyed blond who smelled of stale sweat; getting picked up by a Bosnian banker in a fabulous suit and during dinner realizing from the identity card he showed me (he'd forgotten it indicated marital status) that he was married; in Madrid, a fling with a journalist twenty years my senior who said he had never slept with the love of his life, a woman taking care of her aged parents in Galicia. Once, during sex, when I let him know I wasn't satisfied, he looked me in the eyes and said, "You want this to be like the movies." I did, having no other template. *The Umbrellas of Cherbourg*, not *Last Tango in Paris*.

The last six months, in Stuttgart, had been as devoid of romance as the streets of that city were empty of people on Sundays. But the British students with whom I'd shared a large and airy apartment were wonderfully fun. I remained close

to one of them until she died many years later. "Friendship,"
C. S. Lewis wrote, "has no survival value; rather it is one of
those things which give value to survival." Not having siblings, I especially cherished friends, cultivating them with
letters and visits, and mourning when our paths diverged.
Romance is even less necessary, perhaps, than friendship.
And romance can verge on obsession. I knew that madness
because I'd fallen in love with a student in college. I'd asked
the resident adviser who introduced us, "Is Rick gay?"

"No," she said. "Why do you think that?" What could I
say? That he was gentle and gracious, that his apartment was
stylish, that he didn't have a girlfriend despite being tall and
handsome. And why did I let myself believe her? Loving him
consumed my college years, but when I finally cut that ribbon of bewilderment and unrequited desire, I turned my love
into a bow of friendship.

By Christmas, I was a good, even very good, waitress. I paid
attention to details: who needed water or a clean ashtray. I
liked proving Frau Steffen wrong. I liked making change from
my red wallet, fast, fast, fast. And friendly, friendly, with my
wide American smile. That smile when approaching every
table would be seen as odd, even suspicious, in a German. It
was as if I opened a window in the room simply by being who
I was, but I didn't know that as much as I just felt the outside
air. I thought my coworkers felt it too but didn't recognize it
as a positive thing. I was the only American worker in the village, something I learned when the Steffens told me about an
Australian working in a day lodge higher in the mountains.
"Perhaps you can meet her," Frau Steffen said. And while the
villagers did not ask to touch my hair, as they did of James
Baldwin when he lived in Leukerbad in the early 1950s, and

while I did not have dark skin, I was clearly not of this place. Why did Americans smile all the time, I wondered—perhaps it is the physical manifestation of our boundless, often misguided optimism. There's a Russian proverb: "Laughing for no reason makes you a fool."

At the end of each night, we paid Frau Steffen for what we had ordered, according to the chits we filled out, and for any mistakes. One night I came up forty francs short. It was 11:30 p.m. and our legs were swollen and our backs aching. I felt the pressure to pay. Instead, I said, "I'm going to count my orders again." My coworker rolled her eyes. Frau Steffen tapped the bar with her pen.

I took the chits in my pile, looked at the handwriting, and recalled the guests out loud. I got to a chit for forty francs and held it up for Frau Steffen and the other waitress. "This is not my handwriting."

My coworker shrugged as if to say, *It was worth a try.* I looked at Frau Steffen, but her face was merely weary.

A year before, in Paris, while working as an office temp, I'd shoplifted an umbrella (red matryoshka dolls on a black background and a carved walnut handle), a Caron scarf (a gift for a friend), and a bar of vetiver soap from the Galeries Lafayette. Those thefts impressed themselves in my memory: Why had I done it? Perhaps I was motivated by a sense of being neglected and undervalued. The Paris job involved answering the telephone for a man whose secretary was on vacation. Filing forms that no one would ever consult again. If I didn't come to work, my boss would answer—or let ring—his own phone. At least at the Eigerblick we were necessary. *Stuff*, pretty stuff, made you feel better. Maybe taking something that belonged to someone else also made you feel better, especially if you thought that person had something she didn't deserve. Maybe my coworker saw me as lording my lark of a winter season over her. She was working at the Eigerblick because that was all she could do, and she would be a waitress for a long time.

I felt a protective sheath thicken around me. Local subsistence farmers, idle during the winter, often sat at a round table, a Stammtisch, drinking beer or Swiss wine or one apple brandy after another, frequently mixed with coffee. *Gruezi mitenand*, I learned to say. Frau Steffen gave them every fifth drink free, bantered about the weather, and batted her eyelashes, hoping they felt at home at the Eigerblick or that they at least would keep buying her alcohol. I sensed they didn't like her. Or me. Or the Swiss girls. The farmers seemed to resent the tourist industry, as though we were ruining their village with our outsider values and our commerce. Their leisure was the result of the weather, not extra income.

Unlike France or Germany, where some family names retain a "de" or "von" indicating landowning nobility, Switzerland is more homogeneously bourgeois. Until the twentieth century it was a country of subsistence farmers. The men at the Stammtisch were clinging to a way of life superseded when capitalism blossomed, alongside the idea that institutions such as universities and banks, not princes, should manage people and resources.

The hotel had depressingly ordinary furnishings, as one might expect of a rental property, but we did a decent lunch and dinner business from people who stayed at better places. Tired of Dover sole parisienne with potatoes Anna at the Hotel Regina, they came to us for the stunning view and simple Swiss food. At the Eigerblick, only breakfast was included. I overheard the Steffens arguing about whether to increase revenue by requiring guests to eat dinner there.

"I can't do it with Paul alone," he said, his voice rising in anger.

"Being busier would keep you from getting drunk," she hissed. Then a door slammed.

Unlike chic resorts such as St. Moritz or Gstaad, Grindelwald was a town for serious skiers. That winter, our guests included athletic and well-heeled Americans, Swiss, English, Spaniards, Italians, Japanese, and a lot of northern Germans. The Germans seemed intrigued by me: born in Munich, the child of two parents displaced by World War II, a Silesian mother and Slovenian father. I was not completely American, but neither was I European. A few guests mistook me for a Yugoslav until I opened my mouth and US-accented German came out. My family's immigration to New York City represented the American dream—we arrived with nothing, and twenty years later our middle-class status was regained, thanks to my parents' work, which also resulted in a college education for me. Social mobility used to be much less possible in Europe. My father and I couldn't even attain German citizenship—not that he wanted it, having fought against the Germans in the war. Until we became US citizens, we were officially stateless.

Historian Jürgen Kocka distinguishes between the bourgeoisie of property and that of culture: either can be a route to the middle class. The Steffens had neither. Frau Steffen had the air of someone destined for a better life and thus an aura of continual disappointment. Perhaps her parents had been confident that her unusual beauty would attract a wealthy husband and saw her marriage as an economic step down. Perhaps she had married a charming, happy-go-lucky older man in defiance and now regretted it. Frau Steffen might have finished high school, but not with good enough grades to admit her to the university. There were few options for women who didn't do well in school. Women didn't get the right to vote in federal elections in Switzerland until 1971.

Through contact with guests I overcame my introversion. I asked questions, another American trait. "What part of Germany are you from?"

"From Danzig, but we live in Bremen now," replied the well-groomed German man. He and his wife lingered over coffee after breakfast, and I sensed they welcomed conversation with me.

"Like Günter Grass?" I hadn't read *The Tin Drum*, or anything by Günter Grass, for that matter, but I pretended to have read certain books, partly as self-inflation and partly to connect with people.

"Yes," said the wife, "we were refugees too."

"My mother was from Breslau." We used the German names for cities that were ceded to Poland after the war. The names were code words of loss. "I've never been to northern Germany," I continued.

The husband smiled. "You must go to Bremen someday. The bombs spared the beautiful medieval center, called the *schnoor* because the houses appear as on a winding piece of thread." After World War II, most German cities were rebuilt from complete ruins with numbing similarity: pedestrian market centers with crisp cobblestones, white curbs, and gleaming churches. Perhaps the German guests liked me because they, too, were irritated by Swiss superiority, Swiss confidence that everything can be managed, including the avoidance of conflict.

I'd had plenty of jobs—cleaning houses, secretarial work, cooking—but until that winter I'd never had a job requiring me to bifurcate myself so strongly. I enjoyed my ability to charm guests and read their psyches. But the moment I left the energy of the dining room I deflated; I was a life raft with the air let out. I kept reminding myself that the winter wouldn't last forever. American psychologist Angela Duckworth argues that "grit" gears someone for success. Her signs of grit—such as accountability and perseverance—are standard German behavior. My double consciousness resonated in other ways. The American Revolution, of course, was a bourgeois revolution, one whose progressive values I had absorbed, but in lockstep with the German value of reliability, where one does not dream of "blowing off" a responsibility or a rendezvous. Between my American optimism and my German determination, I didn't consider quitting.

Years later an American friend of mine would marry a wealthy man, so wealthy he'd never shopped for his own clothes—wardrobes were brought to his parents' New York apartment for him to choose from. For the first time, being married to my middle-class friend, he was obliged to carry money. Each night, he threw his change into the trash. This appalled me, and I jokingly offered to come pick it out, but my friend said that when her husband wasn't looking, she did exactly this. Their marriage, containing such different values, was doomed.

Perhaps those who have to face real conditions of life—to use Marx's criterion for the bourgeoisie—are happier. Where does one's sense of self come from, if not from something one has made or done or earned? Eventually one must realize, Emerson writes, that "no kernel of nourishing corn can come to [a person] but through his toil bestowed on that plot of ground which is given to him to till." The statement applies to people who can and want to toil. Others happily consume corn without toiling. I hadn't yet identified my plot of ground, but I did toil, good practice for the future.

Frau Steffen economized by hiring three seasonal waitresses instead of four. I saw that this could increase my tips. Most people rounded up the bill, leaving twenty francs for a bill of nineteen. Each night in my pine-paneled room, I stacked the small half-franc silver coins pressed with garlands and the word *Helvetia* and a statue that reminded me of Liberty. I admired the hundred-franc note with Borromini on it. He was born in Ticino, but his most famous buildings were in Rome, the city Ursula and I decided to visit after my season's work. The self-taught Borromini created buildings that convey spontaneous emotion, in part via trompe l'oeil, making apparently moving façades or corridors that looked longer than they were. I'd studied and visited Borromini's buildings: Sant'Ivo alla Sapienza, the church of the University of Rome, with its oval chapel, and San Carlo alle Quattro Fontane, a tiny jewel of a church with a serpentine façade. On my first visit to San Carlino, the octogenarian caretaker led my friend and me to the cloister, stopping to pick two blood oranges from courtyard trees. It was the first time I'd ever eaten an orange straight from a tree, and the red interior, only hinted

at by the ruddy skin, was another surprise. In Italy the exterior does not have to match the interior, a variation on
la bella figura. The appearance *is* the reality. Every time a
hundred-franc note passed through my fingers, I imagined
myself drinking blood orange juice in the Piazza Navona,
wearing short sleeves in the sun in a city where work is less
important than art.

In his book *The Theory of the Leisure Class*, Thorstein
Veblen writes, "Higher learning remained in some sense a
by-product or by-occupation of the priestly classes." My art
history reading was not economically useful, but I'd been in-
doctrinated into a religion of style. Ironically, much of the art
I'd studied was commissioned because of religious fervor. My
parsimony had a higher purpose, I told myself, as I served
food that I knew to be mediocre.

The Eigerblick house specialty was Geschnetzeltes ("chopped
up") Hong Kong, sautéed pork bits with canned fruit cocktail
and a curried cream sauce, served with rice and garnished
with a Chinese paper umbrella. I felt ashamed to serve it,
the heavy cream, the curry powder, the canned maraschino
cherries in the cocktail, a mishmash of Indian and Chinese
and Swiss. Herr Steffen's cooking was untrained and unre-
fined. But the cheese fondue, made with Fribourger vacherin
and gruyère, was heavenly, a treat we were permitted only on
Christmas Eve, when the dining room was closed. Walking
into a cheese store and smelling a whiff of that raw, whole-
some, yet slightly putrid smell brings it all back.

The Swiss probably drink more milk and eat more gooey
melted cheese—including in raclette, where melted cheese
is scraped onto boiled potatoes—than other Europeans.

There's even Rivella, a sparkling soft drink made from whey. Dairy products contain casomorphins that some people say act like opiates. Rather than being drugged into complacency, however, the Swiss are hypervigilant. Every man between the ages of twenty and forty is a soldier, required to retrain annually. There are enough nuclear fallout shelters for each inhabitant and tons of stockpiled explosives. Were the country to be invaded at any of its three thousand points of entry—bridges or roads or tunnels—those points could be blasted to smithereens by a centralized command.

I always had the sense, living in Switzerland, that I was not privy to information shared by everyone else, information buried as deep as those explosives. This tacit understanding ensnared everyone like a web, but there was no way a foreigner could put it all together. The Swiss breathe their ideologies as we US citizens breathe ours, and part of their ideology is a sense of superiority. I would come to recognize this superiority many years later when I moved to Utah. Mormons believe they alone will enter the highest tier of heaven, with the result that they treat everyone else with varying degrees of disdain. Institutionalized in the church, disdain is sometimes personalized as pity.

The Steffens also employed a Serbian couple in their early thirties. They had worked for the Steffens in Ticino. Florika, who was short and fat and smelled of sweat, cleaned rooms and did laundry and helped take care of the two Steffen children. Paul was gaunt, with acne scars. He cooked with Herr Steffen, washed dishes, and shoveled snow.

From her pocket Florika took a dog-eared photo of the two children she and Paul had left in the care of grandparents.

I recited the few Slovenian words that I knew, hoping they were close to Serbo-Croatian: *dobra dan, podgana, nasvidenje* (good day, rat, goodbye), and I counted my change out loud: *ena, dve, tri, štiri, pet.* As if I'd told a joke, she laughed the warm laughter of camaraderie. The hierarchy of Europe's three kinds of root stock—Teutonic, Alpine, and Mediterranean—is clear: the blonder the better. Dark-haired Paul and Florika recognized my family name to mean "soot" in Slovenian—one of my ancestors was a chimney sweep—but they also knew that my father's region had been part of the Austro-Hungarian Empire, and the fact that he'd graduated from the military academy meant he had more of a chance than they did to thrive in a foreign country. He spoke six languages, five of them fluently. They spoke Serbo-Croatian and broken German.

As a gesture of friendship, Florika offered to do my laundry even once I moved out. I knew Frau Steffen would not like it, but I acceded. We were folding sheets by holding opposite corners, dancing a little as we moved toward each other, laughing when we touched fingers, when Frau Steffen walked in on us. "I don't want to see you in the laundry room again," she said to me. She patronized Florika but also befriended her. Frau Steffen's tone of voice with Florika was unlike her tone with us waitresses or with her husband. It had a tender sincerity, solicitousness. It was like the relationship between a queen and a lady's maid. Or a mother and child, even though they were the same age. In retrospect, I realize that Frau Steffen, despite having her children with her, was lonely, and she was obviously working as hard as we were.

Forty years ago, guest workers in northern Europe and Switzerland were mostly from southern European countries with weaker economies. These southern Italians, Greeks, Spaniards, and Yugoslavs were dark-haired and dark-eyed like me. How much education they had in their own countries made a difference in how they coped in the new one. In Europe, xenophobia is an obsession, highlighted recently during the Syrian refugee crisis. In the United States, the problem of difference is often reduced to race, although we also adopt suspicion of religious outsiders: Irish Catholics mostly in the nineteenth and early twentieth centuries, Jews and Muslims then and now.

A friend who'd worked in a large Swiss hotel in the 1970s told me that her group of American college students was required to eat with the managers, even though the students were poorly paid. When my friend sat with her coworkers, the Italian chambermaids, she was reprimanded. The Swiss state was supposed to be "born neither of race nor of the flesh but of the spirit," yet in 2014, Switzerland passed a draconian anti-immigration law, a response to foreign labor that refused to go back home. Like the protagonist in the film *Bread and Chocolate*, many workers had done the math of Switzerland's high salaries and preferred exile to insecurity. Half of Swiss voters backed the 2014 referendum to impose quotas on immigration, a response to the fact that a quarter of Swiss citizens were by then immigrants, double the ratio of Germany or the United States.

Like Florika and Paul, I was a guest worker in Switzerland, and my visa, like theirs, was inscribed with precise entry and exit dates. We reported to the police department. But I had applied to US law schools and taken the US Foreign Service exam, and although I didn't know what the future held for me, I knew it would not be another season at the Eigerblick.

Florika and Paul would continue to shuttle back and forth between home and this country that seemed to look down its mountainous nose at them.

Phone calls were expensive. I called my parents only once a month from Frau Jaun's kitchen. I didn't tell them I was miserable. Because of the way they'd struggled during our early years in the United States, and because my father made it clear that the money he earned was his alone to spend, I never wanted to ask for any. Without discussion, my father would buy himself Franklin Mint coins or a new tractor while he gave my mother a pittance to run the household, out of which she had to scrimp spending money for herself.

I received mail at the hotel. "Ha, ha, look at the mighty dollar," Herr Steffen sniggered at the weak American currency when he handed me correspondence from schools I'd applied to or from the State Department about my foreign service interview. My mail was evidence that I would have a future, although the law school letters were almost all rejections. With my only moderately above-average LSAT score, why did I apply to Yale? I'd had no guidance, either in high school or in college, and my parents hadn't a clue about the American system.

A friend sent me a paperback copy of Gabriel García Márquez's *A Hundred Years of Solitude*, and since we had Christmas Eve off, I lost myself in Rabassa's translation, devouring the entire book in one night. *He began to decipher the instant that he was living, deciphering it as he lived it, prophesying himself in the act of deciphering the last page of parchments, as if he were looking into a speaking mirror.* When someone asked Rabassa if his Spanish was up to the task, he replied, "It's my English that you should be worried about." Reading the novel, I thought, *My language is my country.* That language was English. I didn't practice the daily habit of writing, but I wrote many letters to friends. I would be disappointed by the banality of those letters now, no doubt, just as I'm dismayed when I see in photos how fat I looked after three months at the Eigerblick.

Two hundred francs were deducted from our paychecks for food. Employees ate early, in the kitchen: rice with bits of sausage or pasta with tomato sauce or, on especially bad nights, muesli. The kitchen refrigerator had a lock to which only the Steffens had a key. I envied Frau Steffen's *salatteller*—leaf lettuce, cucumbers, grated carrot, and celery root that she enjoyed at a dining room table. We didn't get a fresh vegetable except carrots all winter, and the only fruit was cottony, flavorless, cellared apples. The Steffens were, of course, trying to profit from our diets as well as our labor.

Each morning, the only time my access to food was unrestricted and unobserved, I made myself an ice cream shake with Ovaltine. In college, I'd kept a food diary: 14 M&M's = 71 calories. One strawberry Twizzler = 40 calories. In Grindelwald, I didn't reckon the extra calories I was consuming: chocolate bars in my room, morning milkshakes, and afternoon cake. I was trying to eat my loneliness, or fill it.

Frau Steffen looked at me, disgusted. "What are you eating that you are getting so fat?" My black wraparound skirts started to flap open. My body seemed to belong to someone else.

During holiday weeks and most of February, business was so brisk we couldn't take days off; we would be paid for them when we left. We were on duty either from 7 a.m. to 8 p.m.

or 11 a.m. to midnight, with two hours off in the afternoon. I worked so many hours between Christmas and the beginning of March, I saw Ursula only once. She and I had become friends five years earlier, when she au-paired for the Gallup-Kingsley family and I cooked for the Lovejoys next door in Old Black Point, a community of turn-of-the-twentieth-century summer homes overlooking Long Island Sound. We arranged the same day off, and our friendship blossomed on day trips to Mystic seaport or to the Shakespeare Festival.

That job seemed so *familial* compared with the Eigerblick. I didn't eat with the Lovejoys and I slept in the attic, but they allowed me time to enjoy the beach. They took me waterskiing. They trusted me with a supermarket credit card. Their world of polo ponies, Park Avenue, and Palm Beach put them in the upper class, even though Mr. Lovejoy worked. He was a lawyer. Investments enabled them to give their household employees in New York City and New Jersey the month of August off while they rented a house and staffed it with temporary workers like me. They weren't trying to economize. They hosted their sons and grandchildren in an easy, August-beach-vacation way. They drove a station wagon with battered wood-paneled sides. The food they asked me to cook was simple: baked fresh fish and boiled vegetables and local tomatoes. No dessert.

The American family Ursula worked for, the Gallups, also owned a house in the Bernese Oberland. Ursula had three children to take care of, but she, too, was treated well. We were learning—in my case, cooking, in hers, English—while making a little money. We were also observing the habits of the American upper class, such as the tradition of naming a girl after her mother's maiden name ("Kingsley," for instance) or drinking scotch on the rocks before dinner. Our employers discussed politics and art with ease and depth. The opera singer Frederika von Stade was one Lovejoy son's best friend. Conversely, the Steffens never mentioned art, and Herr Steffen talked about politics as if he were mouthing bumper stickers.

My loneliness turned into contempt for the Steffens and the waitresses, who, by mid-January, were not getting along. I felt a twinge of pity for Suzanne. All winter I was looking up at one of the highest mountains in the Alps while looking down at this dysfunctional group of misfits, including me. Our displacements were partly the cause of that dysfunction, but the other part was economic, struggling to pay bills and working fourteen-hour days.

During my two hours off, I walked to the village, often to the celadon-colored glacier. I wanted to take off my glove, touch the ice, and put my fingers to my tongue, but it was just beyond my reach. I was reminded of José Buendía in García Márquez's novel, who thought a cake of ice was the largest diamond in the world and paid to touch it. Forty years after my winter season, that glacier has melted dramatically, and the Swiss worry about climate change, something they cannot control.

The glacier was near the other hotel that had offered me a job, albeit for one hundred francs less. Larger than the Eigerblick, with wings added to the original building, the Gletschergarten was decorated with wood carvings, painted furniture, and Persian rugs.

"What's it like to work here?" I asked a waitress.

"Chic," she said, meaning a combination of "nice" and "fun." "The hotel's been owned by the same family since the last century." I didn't have the heart to hear more.

Once a week I took skiing lessons, along with an ever-changing group of tourist children. The instructor, in his seventies, called me "Mami," sometimes "Grossmami." He raised an eyebrow when he learned I worked at the Eigerblick.

My ski lessons consisted of learning how to get on and off the various lifts, unbuckle gear, and maneuver poles. It was boring and not at all aerobic, and it exemplified the Swiss mania for *training*, for learning in tiny, laborious steps. It took the entire winter before I was permitted to ski on a real slope. At the end of the season, Ursula met me for an afternoon of skiing. She chose a black slope with a decline so steep that I had to take off my skis and slide down on my butt while she zigzagged down carrying my skis and both sets of poles on her shoulders. I didn't question her choice then. Was she making sure I knew I'd never be as good as she was? Or did she simply miscalculate the value of ten lessons? She had learned to ski when she learned to walk. I thought I would learn to ski that winter, and instead I learned—what *did* I learn? I learned what it's like to be a guest worker in a strange land, and I learned how to cope or fight back—not in a communal, heroic *Norma Rae* kind of way, but in a personal *This is what I need to do to get through* way. You'll be dead soon, I told myself, a Zen-like nugget I'd picked up from a Dick Cavett interview with Maya Angelou.

One afternoon in the dining room, guests were transfixed by the sight of climbers trying to scale the mountain, which looked like a grainy black-and-white photograph, rock poking out from under ice and snow. The climbers were black insects crawling slowly up the white face. Herr Steffen rushed out of the kitchen with binoculars. While we stood, squinting, one spiderlike climber fell, except there was no web to hold him. Everyone gasped. Helicopters attempted a rescue. Later we heard the climber had died. The mountain was nicknamed Mordwand (death wall), a rhyme with Nordwand (north wall). The Greeks considered mountains divine, the home of the gods. Climbing them seemed like hubris to me.

By the third week of March, the number of tourists had dwindled, and Frau Steffen called a meeting of the waitresses. We sat together at a dining room table as though we were guests, the first time since Christmas Eve. Frau Steffen turned to me and asked, "Would you like to end your service this Saturday?" She paused. "You have accumulated enough days off so that I can pay you for the month."

She was being careful, I realized, lest I contact the lawyer again. I had grown used to my indenture, but the timing was right.

To celebrate, Ursula and I took the rail line up to Jungfraujoch, the tallest outlook point in the Oberland and the highest railway station in Europe, at more than eleven thousand feet. It is the site of the chase scene in the James Bond film *On Her Majesty's Secret Service*. Ursula snapped a photo of me, chubby-cheeked, surrounded by white peaks and drifts. (Sadly, even the Ewiger Schnee, snow that never melts, is unnaturally melting now.)

A night later we boarded a train to Rome. The Pensione Terminus, where we stayed, had fourteen-foot ceilings and rooms so large you could roller-skate in them. Run by an Italian in his fifties and his younger German wife, the place had a genteel charm, with furnishings from the 1920s. I imagined the owners had met when she was a tourist.

On the Vatican side of the city, I made sure we found the white granite apartment building of the Roman countess for whom I could have worked as an au pair. I stood on the sidewalk, trying to glimpse life inside the handsome structure. I would have learned Italian, I thought, and maybe even fallen in love, like the woman at the Terminus. I certainly would have eaten better food. But I would not have saved thousands of Swiss francs.

I walked off those twenty pounds in the eternal city and during my subsequent months of travel. Savoring the difference between solitude and loneliness, I visited Greek ruins and Spanish villages. A part of me had hardened, the way cheese left uncovered becomes tough as plastic. I often wonder why that season, such a relatively short time in my life, had such a lasting effect on me. That winter, time passed in the slow and inexorable increments of a melting icicle. Perhaps I realized, although I am able to articulate it only now, that hard work enables one to appreciate the luxury of leisure. And that I had to make my own happiness.

Several summers later, I visited Grindelwald again. Ursula and I had kept in touch, and that afternoon we walked along trails dotted with gentian and speedwell and shepherd's purse, flowers whose names she knew. She carried her first baby in a backpack. We were both married by then, both in bloom with love and adulthood. I'd dropped out of law school, and my foreign service interview had been a disaster, but I had earned a master's degree in writing and discovered I loved teaching, which was a way I could read and talk about

books and call it work. And teaching is not unlike waitressing, wherein the server must figure out what the guest needs,
despite what the guest says she wants.

"I must go up the hill," I told Ursula, as she settled on a
bench to nurse her daughter.

The new management at the Eigerblick hadn't heard of
the Steffens. I walked through the dining room to look at the
north side of the mountain. The winter when I worked there,
the view was like wallpaper for me. I'd only paid attention
to it when humans were climbing the mountain or falling to
their death from it. Now I noticed that the shape was some-
what concave, like half a cone, a shape that put one side of
the mountain in constant shadow, even if the sun was shin-
ing. The shape also made it hard to climb, requiring a rap-
pel almost all the way down. Half the cone was air: thin and
invisible air. Not even ice to hold on to. I imagined holding
on to a rope and facing that wall of inaccessible rock and ice.
Dangling, I wouldn't know that people were watching, that
someone was hoping I would make it.

Auntie

> If the moon looks larger here than in
> Europe, probably the sun does also.
>
> —THOREAU

WHEN I WAS ALMOST FIVE, WE MOVED FROM NEW YORK City into the ground-floor apartment of a house in Roselle, New Jersey. A relic of when the street had horses and carriages, the Victorian house sat close to the now-busy road. Railroad tracks bordered the backyard, and the sound of trains punctuated days and nights. Helen Severs, a childless sixty-six-year-old widow, lived on the top floor. "Call me Auntie," she said. She was shorter than my mother, with sinewy arms and legs that extended from small-print cotton dresses that she wore with brown tie oxfords and sheer stockings. Her close-clipped and thick steel-gray hair was curly with a "permanent." She had returned to New Jersey to be near her sister, after Auntie had found her husband dead of a heart attack on the toilet in their Clearwater, Florida, house. This fascinated me, as I had never seen a dead person and I couldn't imagine what it's like to find one on the toilet, of all things, a place where no one should be seen.

Behavior

In the summer, Auntie and I gathered cornflowers, spiderwort, daisies, and dandelions from empty lots and parking strips for me to make a short-stemmed table arrangement in a juice glass. I pulled the wire shopping cart or held the leash of Mask, her well-trained boxer. "One too many in the kitchen" was his cue to leave the room, no matter which room. But he sat on my command only when Auntie was there.

We were always back at her apartment by 1:30 p.m. for *As the World Turns*. We cooked French toast and macaroni and cheese and chocolate chip cookies, tossing in bonus chips at the end. Buying an extra package of chips to enrich the last cookies seemed luxurious. Auntie taught me to keep my napkin and my hands in my lap (instead of on the table, like my parents did) and to butter my dinner roll in pieces. "It's not a sandwich," she said. And, "Don't lick the ice cream off the spoon in layers." It was my joy to clean Auntie's silver, wiping each piece with a polish-soaked sponge.

"All nice things require some care," she said as she lowered the ironing board so I could iron napkins. But she had no airs about anything, and in retrospect, I realize she owned nothing except the things in her small apartment. Yet her lack of money and higher education were irrelevant to her manners, which came from a deep well of consideration for others.

Card and Board Games and Hobbies

1. Gin Rummy, Parcheesi, Monopoly, Checkers, Poker

"Why can't I end the run with an ace?" I asked. My parents put the ace after the king as well as before the deuce, I was sure.

"We don't do it that way."

"Why not?" I asked, my voice insistent, louder.

"Because those are the rules," Auntie said.

"I don't like the rules," I shouted, and then the phone rang.

Auntie answered. "It's okay," she told my mother. "She's not misbehaving; we're playing a game."

2. Auntie's Florida hobby was ornamenting mirrors and purses with seashells. From her dresser, she took out rolls of cotton filled with plastic bags of small shells: angel wings, lettered olives, cockles, bay scallops, sundials, and slippers. I learned the names and held the shells with my fingers while she squeezed on a bead of glue. Then we placed the shells on what looked like a miniature picnic basket. It was less practical but more calming than my mother's mania for sewing and painting walls and refinishing furniture.

Books

My German grandfather in Uffing sent me *Struwwelpeter*. In the title story of this collection, a slovenly boy who does not brush his hair or cut his nails is shunned by other children. Because my hair was thick and curly, this was my mother's nickname for me, although she made sure I was never slovenly. In other stories, a girl who plays with matches burns to death. A boy who sucks his thumb has it cut off. Hans fails to look where he's walking and falls into the river. Kaspar refuses to eat his soup, wastes away, and dies. The stories appealed to me in all their gruesomeness, missing in American books of the time.

Though it is true enough that everything we do has consequences, the book instilled a fear in me that if we do something bad, we deserve something bad to happen to us. There are no accidents. I learned to be careful although I sometimes refused to eat my mother's tomato soup, thickened with flour.

The starch ruined the taste for me. I sat at the kitchen table staring at a cold bowl of it until my mother tired of watching me and snatched it away. "Go to bed," she said, roughly pulling the chair with me in it out from under the table. She scraped the soup back into the pot. "I starved during the war and you won't eat. Why did God give me such an ungrateful wretch for a child?"

Celebration

Neither my thirty-four-year-old mother nor my forty-seven-year-old father thought to have a party for me—in Europe, children's birthdays were celebrated in the family. But Auntie did, on my sixth birthday, with a bakery cake and ice cream. We played "pin the tail on the donkey" using rubber suction cup darts in her living room, the furniture pushed against the walls. A photograph shows my pale face between those of my best friends, Thomas and his brother, Emmanuel Cristodaro, who had cerebral palsy. In 1961 immigrants were placed in classes with children with disabilities. The party noise probably drove my mother crazy. She would also have been distressed by the mess, which Auntie and I had fun cleaning up together. We established a rhythm. On Fridays after school I headed upstairs with a change of clothes, coming down only on Sunday night. "Are you sure she's not a bother?" my mother asked, the answer clear as the gleam in Auntie's eye.

Dewey Decimal

In second grade in Indiana, where we moved because of my father's job offer from Studebaker, standardized test results placed me in the gifted class. During recess, my classmates asked me to teach them German. They ran back into the classroom saying *guten morgen* to one another and calling out *rot, grün, blau, weiss*. For the first time, I felt that my immigrant status was more interesting than odd. We created a supermarket out of empty cans, boxes, and plastic fruit, and we learned to weigh produce and make change. I loved school so much that I tried to hide, successively, the symptoms of measles, mumps, and chicken pox. On the toy box in my room, I displayed my ten or so books, plus books borrowed from the library, and my own animal stories with construction-paper covers and hand-sewn bindings. Rocks were bookends. I alphabetized by author and taped index cards inside the back covers so that patrons (my parents and my stuffed animals) could borrow them.

Displacement

In winter, snow covered the doors and windows of South Bend. It was like being smothered. In my three years in Indiana, Auntie and I talked on the phone often, and we saw each other when she visited us and when I visited her during the summers.

Then the Studebaker plant closed and my father joined Mercedes-Benz of North America, which was building a headquarters in New Jersey. As in the move to Indiana, my father bought a house without my mother or me seeing it first. On the drive to our new house my mother asked me to read a theater marquee. I couldn't see the letters to read it. Later I learned about a theory that children develop bad eyesight when there's something they don't want to see. What didn't I want to see? That my father could, and would, decide everything? One good thing about moving was that Auntie and I no longer needed to fly seven hundred miles to see each other. The Victorian house had been torn down, but she was living in an apartment around the corner from her sister, a forty-minute drive from our new town.

Excelsior

"You can throw away that excelsior," Auntie said. I'd never heard the word before, and rarely since. It sounds like a mix of "excellent" and "superior" but refers to something cheap. I couldn't find it in the dictionary because I looked under x. A trademarked word for wood shavings, once used to fill mattresses, then as packing in boxes. How strange to coin a word for something that can already be named. How American to make it sound special. To commodify it.

The Freys

One summer afternoon, surrounded by three generations of Auntie's family (her sister Bertha and husband, Fred; their four grown children and spouses; and their grandchildren), I wore a brown, green, and red plaid dress made by my mother. The scoop neck had half an inch of lace ribbon sewn into the seam and around the short sleeves. With a white apron, it could have been a dirndl. I felt the honor of Auntie having chosen me, different from her love for her family.

I knew the older generation because of poker nights, when I played Auntie's hand with her, the only child there. Sometimes she had a whiskey sour that I got to taste. Upstairs, the Freys' small 1920s house smelled of mothballs, downstairs of cake. It was crowded with old and comfortable upholstered and slipcovered chairs and couches. A glassed-in front porch had wicker furniture and stacks of the *Daily News*, *TV Guide*, and women's magazines.

One of the men grilled hot dogs and hamburgers to be placed in soft white buns that seemed exotic because we ate rye bread at home. A folding table held side dishes. I was mad for the orange gelatin with grated carrots, canned crushed pineapple, and tiny marshmallows.

A boy my age, ten, was whispered to by an adult and I was invited to play ball. I felt awkward, so instead I brought dirty dishes into the kitchen and gathered paper napkins for the trash. I liked the sound of the wooden screen door as it slammed. Being around this large American family, assimilated for generations, reminded me that my family was just my parents and me and our strangeness.

Grandmother Hypothesis

Anthropologists point to grandmothers—or their substitutes—as fundamental to human evolution, filling in the gap between a child's weaning and independence, and contributing to our species' economic productivity. I am not the only immigrant child who benefited from a stranger's care. My friend Jackie mentors a girl she has known since birth. Her Bulgarian parents, neighbors at the time, overwhelmed by having to negotiate medical care and schools for a child born with brittle bone syndrome, relied on Jackie for babysitting and medical research.

Auntie took eleven-year-old-me on a train trip to visit her niece in Maryland. The midcentury modern house in the woods shines in my memory: a house that couldn't be seen from the road, a house filled with books and a piano, too. Jackie took thirteen-year-old Didi to Washington, DC, for a lesson in democracy that included hearing oral arguments at the Supreme Court and meeting Ruth Bader Ginsburg in chambers. It might not "take a village" to raise a child, but in a culture that emphasizes parents and peers, the consistent and loving presence of one stranger is an unforgettable gift.

Inmost

I washed Auntie's hair in the kitchen sink with the spray attachment using Prell shampoo—a pearl suspended into the bottle of thick green stuff. A clean soapy smell, not like flowers or herbs. I wrapped her hair around bristled curlers, painted on setting lotion, and positioned her head under the hair dryer with its inflatable pink hood. She took her hearing aids out first, little machines the size of walnuts requiring batteries that constantly needed changing. Before antibiotics, Auntie had suffered an infected mastoid bone.

We soaked her hands in warm water with a drop of Palmolive dish detergent, just like the commercial showed us, then I cut the nails and let them dry. Then filed them with emery boards. Then polished with pink Sally Hansen polish, a pink that was neither too pale nor too bright. April tulip pink. The pink of her dentures. The fizzy tablets in the blue plastic case. Soaking overnight. The pink plastic imitation of the roof of the mouth. The glue that never worked, affecting speech. A slight click in Auntie's mouth when her dentures were in and a slur when they were not. Brushing out her hair after it dried was like cutting into a frosted cake.

With our TV dinners (my favorite was fried chicken with the square brownie) on TV trays, we watched the Mets. Auntie cheered so energetically she rubbed out two foot-sized ovals on the beige wall-to-wall in front of the TV. I learned to respect a game where the only violence is between a bat and a ball. Where a player can walk between bases and score a run.

Then I got into my pajamas and slept in Auntie's full-size bed. She snored. Past participle of Latin *intimare*: "impress, make familiar," from *intimus*, "inmost."

Kinesthesia

In the seventh and eighth grades, I was bullied by a couple of girls from the "slow" class who wore dirty clothes and lots of makeup. One held the girls' bathroom door closed so no one else could enter while the other threw water and garbage on me over the stall door or as I was trying to exit. They didn't care if they were late to class. I told the assistant principal, who shook his head, but nothing changed. The girls walked home in my direction. To avoid them I took Wyckoff Avenue—a busy street lined with strip malls. When I chose the less crowded and more direct Prospect Avenue, they sometimes followed me, and in the tunnel under the railroad tracks, a tunnel that stank of urine, with broken lights and broken glass, the girls positioned themselves at each entrance, armed with towels soaked in filthy water. They ran up behind me to hit my legs and back with the towels. I stood frozen in the middle as they established their dominance over me. I didn't tell my parents. I didn't tell the school. I was embarrassed to be vulnerable.

"For nonconformity the world whips you with its displeasure," writes Emerson in "Self-Reliance." I didn't know how to conform. I wasn't sure what prompted the bullying, perhaps an amalgam of my foreignness and good grades. Despite the bullying, however, I experienced no depression, no loss of interest in school, no health complaints. If my parents' focus on me was the raw wool of my childhood, the weft was my rebellion against them, and the warp was Auntie's steady presence, weaving me into a person who determined her own self-worth.

Maternity

I knew that Auntie's lack of children of her own made her sad, that she was wistful about her sister's luck. When we first met, she encouraged me to "pray for a little brother or sister." Grateful that prayers could be silent, I did not pray for a sibling. I enjoyed my status as "only." I didn't play with dolls, and I didn't play "house." In fact, I disliked being around children younger than I was, but I realized early that this was unusual in a girl and that I should not advertise it. I also didn't babysit except for a couple of Saturday nights for my father's German boss and his wife, Anneliese. When Anneliese asked me to watch their two sons while she went skiing during Christmas break, I agreed because I understood that I helped define my father's status as a good employee.

At Anneliese's house that morning, I was confronted with three more women standing in the kitchen, surrounded by six children, four more than I'd ever cared for. My heartbeat quickened. I wanted to object, but I worried about jeopardizing my father's relationship with his boss. Or my parents' social life?

"Give them hot dogs for lunch, and there's baby food in the fridge," Anneliese said, as she and her friends piled into a car, chic in their hand-knit hats and shiny nylon jackets. "We'll be back by four."

Their mothers gone, the children rampaged through the house as if stung by bees. The baby tried to hold herself up by doorknobs and furniture, crying each time she was trampled. Knickknacks tumbled off shelves, bottles in the liquor cabinet rattled, the cat hid.

At the top of the stairs, I caught up with seven-year-old Jan, the oldest. Grabbing his wrist, I said, "Stop. Someone will get hurt."

"No, we won't," he yelled, using his free hand to throw a bath towel down the stairwell. It landed on a child's head below. A peal of laughter.

I tightened my grasp. "I'll call your father."

He looked at me with disgust. But he stopped struggling and we went down the stairs. The other children saw his resignation and fell quiet.

I herded them into the large playroom with its sliding glass doors that led to the yard. Within minutes, a child picked up a baseball bat and started swinging. I tore it out of his hand and hid it behind me, alert to the dangers they posed to each other and themselves.

At lunchtime, I took the baby (and the bat) with me. I closed the playroom door and pushed a heavy chair against it, trapping the rest of the children inside. Trying not to breathe in the stink, I changed the baby's diaper. I heated her food and tried to feed it to her, but she sealed her lips tight. From the playroom, there were yells and thumping.

I carried a tray of food and drinks into the playroom. The baby reached for a hot dog, but I'd read about toddlers choking on them and didn't let her have it. She howled. We went back to the kitchen where I minced a piece of hot dog for her. She refused it.

For the rest of the afternoon, I watched the children from my position by the door of the playroom. I imagined telling the mothers, "You're lucky no one died." Why would anyone put themselves through the torment of being responsible for other lives, I wondered. Doctors save people at controlled intervals called "work," but I could not imagine the weight of responsibility for a child's well-being twenty-four hours a day, year after year after year. How could mothers go skiing? How could they sleep?

When the women returned, cheeks flushed from fresh air and sun, they hurried to retrieve their children and leave. No one asked about my day. Anneliese did ask me to wait until her husband could give me a ride home—another hour. I sat on the couch and read magazines, trying to unwind my hypervigilance. I vowed never to babysit again. When Anneliese paid me, I stared at the five-dollar bill: the same seventy-five cents an hour I earned babysitting her two sons on Saturday nights.

Boys didn't babysit back then, just as girls didn't cut grass. The women would not have taken advantage of an adult babysitter, except perhaps for a recent, brown-skinned immigrant. The horrible day lodged in my head the fact that I couldn't trust women to be fair to me simply because we were both female.

Questions

Writing this, I get in touch with Auntie's great-grandnephews and -nieces to ask if they found it strange that I bonded with their great-aunt. They don't remember me. Before he died, I should have asked my father about how he felt working for the Germans he'd fought against. Before her Alzheimer's, I should have asked my mother if she ever disobeyed my father. I have no questions for Auntie. I knew her beyond language, beyond remembering her soapy Blue Grass perfume and her dentures. The shape of her heart matched exactly the emptiness in mine.

The Late Show

I saw Auntie only on some weekends, or for a week or two in the summer. She went to bed before me, and I slept on the sofa bed in the living room. I watched the 11:30 p.m. movie, *Desiree* or *Forever Amber,* the film version of a book I read on my mother's recommendation (she no longer remembered the titillating plot, the rise of a sexual adventuress and mistress to Charles II).

The strongly scented blue-green powder of Spic and Span dissolved into warm water and burned my hands as I washed Auntie's floors. I then polished them with Johnson's wax, rubbing in brown goo and taking pleasure in the shiny result. And I cooked for Auntie, baked chicken and rice, and chocolate chip cookies. At seventeen, it wasn't fun to spend time with an increasingly feeble old woman, but I felt the obligation and my mother reminded me of it. I let Auntie win at checkers.

Where Are You From?

A few days before I turned eighteen, and the same night that I graduated from high school, Auntie died, although I didn't find out until a few days later. She left me her almost-new mattress and box spring, three hundred dollars cash, her mahogany secretary (care of my mother), and a gold and diamond pin. Auntie had worked as a bookkeeper at the Metropolitan Life Insurance Company. After twenty-five years, she got a gold pin, the company name stamped on a gold ribbon swirling over the top like a war medal; every ten years, she got another gold bar connected with gold chain; at fifty years, a half-carat diamond. After college, I had a jeweler work the gold into a ring with the stone and gave it to my mother. I was too young for a diamond, I knew from reading etiquette books.

Auntie also left me a large, ornately framed photo of her at age eighteen. The black-and-white photo with pastel high-lights hangs in my study. Her long, thick hair is pulled into a bun at the back of her neck. Her skin is heavily powdered. She is no beauty, but there's tenderness in her eyes. She wears a bare-shouldered, silk chiffon dress and offers the camera a demure and sidelong glance: before she married, long before she met me, a young woman on the verge of life.

When people ask where I'm from, I could say "Auntie." I could show them the ring that my mother wore. I could say I am from Auntie as if she were a tree and I a bird nesting on strong branches. In those green leaves, I found safety, accep-tance, and love. I learned to fly from a nest so high up no one noticed it.

X, Y, and Z

Helen Severs, née Vollmer, April 8, 1895
  m. John A. Severs 1918
  d. June 1, 1973

"Do you know what this is?" he asked from behind the prep counter, holding up a ripe orange mango blushed with red. His accent mixed Jamaican and Cockney, a glottal stop at the end of "what," the *th* in "this" almost a *d*. We were separated by stainless steel in the steamy hotel kitchen where servers were yelling for orders, cooks were yelling "PICK UP."

I'd spent two years in Europe after college, including one in Paris, where mangos were plentiful. "Of course," I said, stopping to face him. I wore a brown seersucker blouse with a name tag. He cut a slice of the peeled mango and extended it on his palm. I took it, not just because refusing would be rude, but because my eyes drank in the triangle of satiny, espresso-colored neck exposed by the folded-back corner of his white chef's uniform. His fine features, lips no fuller than mine, revealed Scottish and Arawak Indian heritage.

"I'm Tyrone," he said. "People call me Terry, too."

Throughout my childhood and adolescence, my father called black people "duzzum" or "jungle bunnies" or, sometimes, "niggers." Did he pick up these terms from the US Army in

Germany? On the street in New York? From coworkers? Was
he trying to fit in? In my algebra class on April 5, 1968, I re-
marked that King was "another hoodlum." Why did I parrot
my father? My teacher said, firmly, "Dr. Martin Luther King
was not a hoodlum, and we should all be sorry he was murdered." I felt ashamed and resolved to pay more attention to
who was who. Not long after, I read *The Feminine Mystique*
and *The Autobiography of Malcolm X*. When my father used
racial slurs, I asked, "Why do you talk that way?" His racism
and his view on the Vietnam War (we needed to vanquish
communism) shaped me, in opposition. As did my mother's
fear of losing my father's love if she took sides. I never wanted
to be that weak.

There was one mixed-race student in my high school, no
other black kids. While the towns surrounding mine were
also white, New York City had lots of people who were not
white, and I often took the train to go to museums or just
walk around. Skin color presented an otherness more dramatic than my own, a visible and permanent otherness.
Although I wouldn't have been able then to articulate why I
felt more comfortable—even safer—around people of color,
I think now that there was an equity principle involved.
Because I'm female, I know I'm casually considered inferior.
I thought black people might know what that was like and
wouldn't bully me as my father did. If my father found out
that I'd driven the car outside the parameters he'd drawn, he
called me "dreck," dirt. At a Thanksgiving meal many years
later, a friend noted, "Your father talks only to the men at the
table." Repelled by misogyny as deep as his Slavic accent, I
became a feminist. And although I was equally repelled by

racism, I did not see my own. White dominance was a uniform I wore, one that was rarely questioned.

During freshman orientation at the University of Virginia, I met a lanky, black student from Richmond. Sitting on the grass between our dorms, we recommended books to each other, Hugh Prather's *Notes to Myself* and Sylvia Plath's *Ariel*. Later that fall, on our way to hear Eudora Welty read at Randolph Macon College, we stopped for fast food. The woman behind the counter had such a thick southern accent that I turned to my friend for translation. A metaphor, perhaps, for my seeking relationships that could expand the ways I understood the world. I eventually lost my virginity with him, relevant because in my mostly chaste life, Tyrone was the second black man I slept with. Did I fetishize the black body? Yes, I did, I realize as I recall a poem from that time, "Jamaican Rum," an ode to the intoxicating quality of our physical differences. And yet, my attraction was, and still is, to the way people live through their bodies. Tyrone had an easy self-confidence, one that stopped far short of arrogance. His supervisor was a white woman in her twenties with a degree from the Culinary Institute of America. Tyrone winced when she referred to him as "my help" but bowed his head and continued carving a honeydew melon into a swan.

The hotel where we met was in Washington, DC, and when Tyrone drove to New York to see his uncle, he offered me a ride so I could see my parents in New Jersey. In the car, he asked, "If you could go anywhere in the world, where would that be?" I asked questions, too. I had him drop me off on Route 17, partly to save him from going out of his way, but also to avoid allowing my parents to see him. When we shook hands after that four-hour car trip, I wanted to sleep with him. I imagined kissing his strong hands, his smooth face. I liked men without body hair—another equalizing attribute perhaps, or a sign of humanness or even femininity. I had been attracted to women as well as men since puberty, but I hadn't had a sexual relationship with a woman. I think we choose whom to fall in love with, and when. Tyrone's boss at the Hilton kitchen invited me to her birthday party, but I declined, even though I was attracted to her. Maybe a biological impulse also moved me toward a relationship with Tyrone.

At first I told friends that my relationship with Tyrone was about the good sex. What made it good was my ability to let go, to not worry about how I looked or what I said, because I trusted him. He held his knowledge about the world with restraint and patience. I loved that restraint in tandem with his physical strength—he could lift anything, even me. My best friend laughed, "Tyrone looks like he could break a man in two." And I smiled, thinking of myself splayed on the bed, and him running a finger down my naked back.

Entering a swimming pool, a middle-aged white man held the door for me and said, "So, are you going to take my lane?" It was supposed to be a joke. Tyrone would hold the door open, "After you, Madame," and he would be happy to share a lane. My friends noted his charm, saying, "He doesn't have a chip on his shoulder like American black men." I repeated this myself until I realized how wrong it was. Putting nationality ahead of skin color was a way to not confront my own internalized racism. The questioning of Kamala Harris's identity after the 2019 Democratic debates is another example. As the daughter of a Jamaican father and Indian mother, she was

accused by alt-right commentator Ali Alexander of not being
a black American, despite being born and having grown up
in the United States. In other words, parsing the fine points
of any person of color's identity is a maneuver that lets racism win. White Americans don't react the same way to black
people who are not Americans; their guilt is distanced and
abated, they aren't made to admit their dominance.

Tyrone carried his legacy of slavery from growing up in
Jamaica and the UK, from traveling the world, from living in
the United States, and even from his own family. His mother
often praised his younger brother's beautiful light skin. She
expressed that bias, and I expressed mine by emphasizing
Tyrone's foreignness. His accent marked him as an immigrant, and it sometimes gave him a pass in American culture, in the way that Angela Davis was treated with respect
when she spoke French in a shoe store in her hometown of
Birmingham, Alabama. By focusing on nationality instead
of race or power, Americans seek opportunities to ignore
inequity.

I have an indefinite answer to the question, "Where are you
from?" So did Tyrone, who came to London from Jamaica to
join his parents when he was fifteen, after spending his early
teens with an aunt, uncle, and cousins in rural St. Mary Parish.
At sixteen, he'd finished mandatory schooling. With his talent for imagining and then building structures, he could have
been an architect or a sculptor, but he was also dyslexic, and a
working-class, black immigrant. That meant a job. He wanted
to see the world, and the only opening in the British Merchant
Navy was for a galley boy. Eventually, the navy sent him to
cooking school, twice, and he climbed the ranks to executive
chef, usually the only black man on a ship. On these ships he

learned that white men liked to call him "Terry," an English nickname. In South African and Australian ports, police assumed he was indigenous and repeatedly roughed him up, even jailing him until his white shipmates retrieved him. With the navy, he'd spent time in Houston, Los Angeles, and New York, so he was under no illusions about the United States, but since the advent of container shipping, the interesting weeks in exotic ports turned into stopovers of a mere twenty-four hours. Because of cousins in DC, Tyrone eventually landed there and, undocumented, started over again as a line cook.

Tyrone was thirty-six, I was twenty-three when we met. The same number of years' difference between my parents' ages. But not the same dynamic, not at all. Our relationship balanced the power between us, a seesaw that didn't often thump to the ground, leaving one of us stuck. If he was wiser and more mature, he was also more passive. I was willful and dominant. Tyrone was hurt by my bluntness, as when I'd state, "That shirt doesn't look good on you." I prized directness as truth-telling, and it drove me crazy that he wouldn't say what he thought. He avoided confrontation, for instance by not calling me to tell me he couldn't make it from DC to my student apartment in Baltimore, where I was earning a one-year master's degree. After waiting for an hour or more, I would fume, then worry, and then fume again. We treated each other the way we ourselves liked to be treated. He was okay with plans hovering indefinitely in the future. I liked to know, even bad news. Yet despite this friction, we stayed together. Cupid is sometimes depicted as a blindfolded child. My inner child saw what I needed: to love and to be loved unconditionally, madly. The kind of love that makes a bonfire of the debris of the past, with its rejections and disappointments.

A year and a half after that first drive, Tyrone and I rented a four-room row house in southeast DC. I was the only white person on the block. On Sunday mornings, the retired couple across the narrow street put speakers in their upstairs windows and broadcast gospel radio directly into our house. I closed the windows and wore earplugs. My suburban aunt visited once, in the daytime, noting the plastic chrysanthemums in neighbors' window boxes as if she were doing an anthropological study of class. "My surgeon was black," she said. Then she paused. "But a cook?"

My parents never visited. They had retired to a Blue Ridge mountaintop in Virginia where their neighbors proclaimed, "We love it here 'cause there ain't no chiggers and there ain't no niggers." Monthly phone calls began pleasantly. My mother then handed the phone to my father, and the call ended with one of us angrily slamming down the handset. "Go ahead," I said, when he told me he was leaving his money to the Baptist home down the road. My parents didn't care about religion, so the detail was almost funny. Yet disapproval smoldered through the phone wires like burnt garlic. It was obvious to Tyrone that my father disapproved of our relationship, but Tyrone also knew how to wait, another quality that attracted me to him, along with his willingness to change his mind. "I don't really like cats," he said, but a week after I insisted that we adopt one, he was walking around the house with the kitten draped happily around his neck like gray cashmere.

Tyrone held within himself a reserve that no one could touch, not even me. If I developed in antagonism to my father, he developed in antagonism to his mother. After he talked to her in Jamaica, he closed the door in a foul mood, perhaps because of his guilt. She and Tyrone's father were raising his son, Adrian, abandoned by the mother while Tyrone was at sea. Although he supported his son financially, Tyrone knew him only from occasional visits. Tyrone didn't talk about his responsibilities as a father with me. His parents were also raising three of his much younger brothers, born after his parents returned to Jamaica from London. His mother—never without a job or a business or both—hustled on their behalf, arranging DC schools and work for them. She asked Tyrone to buy them air tickets, but after he did, his siblings returned to Kingston within a month. Tyrone shook his head over his brothers' lack of grit. He preferred to love his mother from a distance of fifteen hundred miles in the way a tree might love a hurricane. And she loved him the way the hurricane loves its eye, the still center.

The row house we rented was owned by a legal secretary who speculated in real estate, hoping to fund her retirement. A white woman in her forties, our landlady bought and was renovating another house on Capitol Hill. We paid $380 monthly rent. Built in 1913, the house had been cheaply updated. All the windows, even the bathroom skylight, had bars—which Tyrone asked the landlady to remove. He told me he felt like a caged animal. She said, "Why don't you wait a few weeks and then let me know?" Upstairs, the pistachio and brown shag carpeting was three inches high. Downstairs, ebony-stained wood floors, exposed brick walls, and the original working fireplace gave the space charm. We placed Tyrone's Argentine sword on the mantel and under it his carved wooden statue from Thailand, African drum, and collection of jazz LPs. I had the notion that if a single white woman could live on D Street, so could we.

In high school and college, I was taught to treat the history of US slavery and racism as a parallel track for a train I did not need to board. I watched it with the disorienting feeling that I was moving, but when it passed, I was standing still. Forty years ago, I thought that the color of Tyrone's skin made him likely to be accepted on D Street and that my choosing him was a "get onto D Street free" card. I'm chagrined to admit that I thought I had proven my lack of racism merely by living with Tyrone. I was vaguely aware that some black men internalized their racist preference for white standards of beauty and chose white women as trophies, but our relationship still felt like a victory over racism. It was a victory with a hollow center because—and I didn't know this then—no matter what I did or said, I profited from the racial power inequity in our culture. I didn't know enough about history to understand why our neighbor might be raising her grandchild, like Tyrone's mother. And I didn't think about what it meant to be part of a community—not just tolerated but trusted, the person you might ask to feed your cat. I didn't try to be that person on D Street. Not because I hadn't watched my parents make friends with every one of their neighbors, but because I didn't even think to try.

As DC was built up beyond its old core in the early twentieth century, developers' deeds included restrictions on selling to Jews and black people. When these restrictions were challenged in court, many white people moved to the suburbs, a flight accelerated by riots after the assassination of Martin Luther King Jr. The Civil Rights Act (which included the Fair Housing Act), passed days after Dr. King's death, was supposed to end segregation. Although it did not, and while income disparity in DC is the highest in the country, the city continued to attract African Americans to jobs in government, resulting in many middle- and upper-class African American homeowners.

The new Capitol Hill Safeway stocked pig hocks and collard greens as well as Häagen-Dazs ice cream and fresh baguettes. A couple—he black Senegalese and she French and white—opened a French bakery nearby. When I decreed an Irish pub "all right," Tyrone said, "You mean it's all white." We played darts there, and we also tried neighborhood bars with only black patrons, but although we were welcomed in both, neither space felt quite right.

"Gentrification" suggests that newcomers push out old-timers, but when property taxes remain affordable, existing owners are not forced to move. Low property taxes underfund public schools, however, so newcomers send their children to private schools, another kind of segregation. Moreover, gentrification destroys existing community bonds, and it can increase crime because people coming and going are not recognized, and because newcomers make wealthier targets for property theft. Still, the only crime I was a victim of was when a ten-year-old boy reached into my pocket while I was standing in line to buy a sandwich. I grabbed his wrist with my five-dollar bill still in it.

On one side of our row house was a burnt-out shell and, on the other, a house inhabited by a woman in her early forties, her toddler granddaughter, and sometimes her son. She seemed to be unemployed. When I came home, she was usually on the front porch with her granddaughter.

"Nice day," she'd say to me. Or, "Spring's on the way."

"Looking forward to it," I replied, slipping my key through the industrial-grade steel bars that protected the front door.

Then, just as I thought I was home free, she would mutter, "white bitch." Getting past her without the invective was like having a winning lottery ticket. I used to tell this story to show how resilient I was. I am telling it now as an example of white fragility—a white person's inability to deal with racial confrontation, no matter how mild.

Our neighbor's fights with her son busted out the upper-floor windows and filled her backyard with shattered glass. The windows were replaced with plastic sheeting and duct tape. Sometimes we heard the child screaming and wondered if we should call social services. We didn't. When I called our neighbor's grandchild "illegitimate," Tyrone asked, "What difference does it make?" I pondered. None? Internalized prejudice is like shit on city streets, except that when you step in prejudice, cleaning it off teaches you something. I didn't realize then that my white privilege trumped every other thing about me. I could walk into Garfinckel's and not be followed by a salesperson. I could drive Tyrone's yellow Pontiac Firebird and not be stopped by the police. We didn't discuss the power inequities in the city and everywhere else, and that created distance between us, but we were both used to being cushioned by silence.

Ludus and Storge

Restaurant work gave me something in common with Tyrone. Because most good restaurants and hotels employed only male servers, I felt lucky to be hired as the only female server at 209½ Pennsylvania Avenue, a restaurant on Capitol Hill, in the last August of Jimmy Carter's presidency. Our uniforms made us look like a Hyannis Port wedding party:

bibbed tuxedo shirts and bow ties. A size-fourteen-neck shirt drooped at my shoulders, and since the gray morning-stripe men's pants were impossible to fit to my hips, I wore a black skirt. The uniforms were one of many things at 209½ that implied a *Town and Country* magazine world. A drink— blonde Lillet, white wine, an orange twist, and fresh mint— was named after Marjorie Merriweather Post's estate in Palm Beach, Mar-a-Lago.

Glossy-haired and manicured Jason, the owner's son, was two years older than I. Jason adapted ideas from *Gourmet* magazine to a prix-fixe menu with four choices for each course. In the summer there was cold lobster salad (five dollars extra); in the spring, soft-shell crabs, looking like large insects, pan-fried.

I started working lunches with Jim, in his early thirties, dark-haired, mustached, and slim. He was the only man at the restaurant in a committed relationship. He had a deep laugh, ears that stood out slightly from his head, and a weak arm from childhood polio. He, too, lived on Capitol Hill, four blocks from the restaurant instead of thirteen. "Dahling," he said, in a mix of Mississippi and Greta Garbo, "Now that you're with us, let's call ourselves *waitrons*." One night he gave me a ride home. "Toto," he quipped, as we passed the burnt-out buildings and empty lots, "we're not in Kansas anymore."

I could balance two plates on my arm without having my fingers touch the rims. But I'd never worked in such a small room. On a glass-shelved étagère, brushed stainless-steel pots held coffee and hot water. Lower shelves contained stacked silverware, cups and saucers, and mauve cotton napkins. On a cake stand on the bar, opposite the painted

wooden Indonesian Garuda and next to a huge vase of flowers, was our version of Maida Heatter's sour cream chocolate
cake. Everything else we carried in from the tiny kitchen.

The eggplant-colored ceiling made the tall, narrow space
seem more intimate. The restaurant used to be a dive-y lun-
cheonette, and when paint chipped from the mauve wall,
a dingy yellow layer was revealed. The dank cellar (with, of
course, rats) housed refrigerators, freezers, shelves of goods,
and a desk. This area could be reached only through two trap-
doors: one outside on the sidewalk, and one in the kitchen.

Jason's mother, who bankrolled the restaurant, chose
the smart décor. "I'm Rochelle Rose," she'd say at the door
on Saturday nights, waving a diamond-encrusted hand.
"Welcome to 209½." If customers dallied after paying, she
stood next to their tables until they got the hint. She wore
sheer silks and satins in copper and green, heavy jewelry,
and delicate shoes. Throughout the evening, she nursed a
single-malt scotch on the rocks. Her voice, like her son's,
hissed—but in a lower key: she smoked Dunhills. Every other
night servers took turns hosting, which reduced our pay, so
we were grateful when Mrs. Rose was there, even as we made
fun of her hair color—the orange-pink of krill-fed salmon.

Because we started work at 4:30 in the afternoon and were
not fed, I was starving by 7:30. Other waitrons ate off customers' plates in the tiny triangular dishwashing room. During
my first shifts, I thought: *disgusting.* But one night I cleared
a plate from a clean-looking woman who had not touched
her two fried zucchini pancakes. Standing in the dish room
with her plate, I lifted one pancake and took a bite. Delicious,
a latke with the added flavors of zucchini and Parmesan

cheese, and just the right degree of greasy. I ate the whole thing, then I ate the other pancake too, standing near the warm mist of the spray arm held by the dishwasher, a young man from Ecuador whom the guys dubbed "the missing link" because of his low forehead and continuous eyebrow. I knew this slur was wrong, but I didn't ask them to stop. I was part of the team.

Soon I no longer cared whose plate I was eating from. I also didn't register to vote and didn't declare my tips. It did not occur to me to care whether Jimmy Carter or Ronald Reagan won because, even though I was living in the nation's capital and waiting on members of Congress, I was disconnected from politics. Before the election, a Republican waiter, biding his time until he started a job as a lawyer, asked me, "Who will you vote for?" When I said "no one," he replied, "Good. We need a few more like you." He voted by absentee ballot in Oklahoma, where his vote counted. I felt negligent, but not enough to do anything. I didn't know what was at stake. I'd returned from Europe assuming the laundry detergent ERA was named after the Equal Rights Amendment, my feminism a consistent—albeit simple—platform. I didn't realize that I needed to act to truly be a citizen.

When Reagan won, our primary customers—lobbyists—became more brazen: "Let's have the Dom Perignon; it's on the taxpayers." The fur coats in our closet multiplied.

I learned the difference between mink and sable, the latter many times more expensive because it is rare, lightweight, and silky, once hunted almost to extinction. Its name in Croatian is *kuna*, also the word for their currency. A tipsy guest took someone else's sable coat from the closet, and half an hour later the owner of the ten-thousand-dollar coat

gasped upon finding only an ordinary brown mink. I worried
that it was my fault, but the next day, the now-sober woman
returned the sable.

I should have been worrying about other things: days after
Reagan was elected, a gunman emptied forty rounds from an
Uzi, killing two men and wounding many others in gay bars
in Greenwich Village. In New York's gay newspaper, a college friend wrote, "For all of us worried that the conservative
backlash in this country would bring about terrible unnamed
things, the future is now." That backlash would include a 60
percent cut in federal aid to local governments. Deregulated
banks. EPA and Energy Department budget cuts. Flourishing
racial discrimination and real estate speculation. Slashed
funding for public-service jobs and public transit. Mentally
ill people turned out on the streets. I should have had a sense
of dread. I should have voted.

Almost everyone who worked at 209½ had a college degree;
many had graduate degrees. Holding up a *New York Times* one
Saturday, a bartender with a political science degree from the
University of Chicago compared it to the *Washington Post*.
"The *Post* isn't confident enough for a front-page human-in-
terest story from Indonesia," he said. "DC's provincial," he
continued. DC was heading for sophistication, however, with
the help of its gay men. A florist named Kenneth Love hosted
at 209½ now and then. He was as dark-skinned as Tyrone,
although not as good-looking. He wore a pair of loafers so
beautiful I asked him to take one off so I could look at it more
closely. "Belgian Shoes," he said, "handmade."

"Would you like a glass of my Veuve Clicquot?" he asked.
Clearly, he wasn't hosting for the $3.10 an hour. Why then?

To be elegant in the public eye, or to attract clients who could appreciate his taste? He scorned bouquets with tight buds and baby's breath. I later found out that he grew up working-class in Anacostia, by then an entirely black quadrant of DC isolated by Route 295 and the river. Kenneth didn't inherit taste. He worked hard at raising himself up, schmoozing with white society. His hunger for acquiring and enjoying fine things was as palpable as the lustrous leather of his shoes.

My friend Russell was the son of an ambassador to two African countries. The only African American student in my MA cohort, Russell was tall and slim with skin the color of light caramel. He had striking eyes, beautiful and large, a high forehead, and a receding hairline. His parents lived in a gracious home off DC's Sixteenth Street, and Russell had attended a Swiss boarding school and Hampshire College. In DC, his job was screening documentaries for PBS. Russell corrected Tyrone's French and questioned his cooking techniques, and behind his back, Tyrone made fun of Russell's nasal voice and his hand flourishes. For my birthday, Russell gave me a small, rolled-steel pâté de foie gras mold, something that I have only ever used for cake. In the early 1980s, to be black and gay was like that graphic depicting either two profiles or a vase. People see one or the other. This is different from seeing a black man and assuming him to be a criminal. While jogging in Chicago, writer Brent Staples whistled opera so women wouldn't be afraid of him. Tyrone wore plain cotton shirts and no jewelry, and he refused to serve watermelon or to fry chicken. How many black men in DC would have recognized a pâté de foie gras mold? I knew three of them.

The restaurant was the inverse of the larger culture: gay waiters and cooks had an automatic pass, while straight men had to prove they weren't homophobic to get hired. Our straight bartender was an actor, comfortable around gay men. The workspace was what theorist Michel Foucault calls a heterotopia—a compensatory place of otherness, valuable for its affirmation of difference and a way to escape repression. We developed a camaraderie with deep roots. With a beer glass as a microphone, the bartender narrated in Marlin Perkins's whisper as the waitrons mimed *Wild Kingdom* animals. Maybe our fun—often at the expense of customers, Jason and his mother, or ourselves—was protection. The ancient Greeks feared laughter; Plato worried it might undermine society. Perhaps our bonding mirth undermined the existing social structure, one that in 1980 still forced queer folk to be closeted to one degree or another. A structure also built on racism, sexism, and classism, but most of us didn't know how to challenge the system through the law. We had no public, active voice.

To fit in at 209 ½, I pretended to know more than I did. I didn't mention the fact that the hotel where I worked in Switzerland used canned fruit cocktail for the pork Hong Kong or that I'd never eaten sweetbreads. My knowledge of wine was limited to reading wine-writer Hugh Johnson's books, but I was sucking up information the way beurre blanc absorbs butter. I tasted the only bread pudding I've ever liked: brioche in an orange-vanilla-flavored custard, rich with egg yolks.

Steven, the only Cordon Bleu–trained chef at the restaurant, made the pudding. "My mother supports an entire African village," he told me. "But she hasn't talked to me, much less given me a cent, since I told her I was gay." It's no wonder that gay folk refer to one another as "family." Most of the gay employees at the restaurant were closeted or estranged from their parents. Given her closeness with Jason, this cast Mrs. Rose in a warm light.

My European background had impressed Jason despite his misogyny. If he had been more mature, I might have sympathized with him for being Jewish in a city where anti-Semitism was as rampant as racism. Although real estate developer Morris Cafritz owned a good portion of the city, his wife, Gwen, renowned for her parties and her art philanthropy, wanted everyone to know she wasn't Jewish. She insisted on being buried in a Presbyterian cemetery rather than in the Cafritz plot in Washington's Hebrew Cemetery. I was only tangentially aware of the interwoven lace of prejudice in DC. Sometimes I'd find a thread loose in my hands, but I couldn't see the pattern.

The waitrons could be as polished as gemstones or as prickly as pickle forks. They taught me to yank open the kitchen door and yell, "HDA" (hairdo alert), so that the cooks could look out the small window or, in exceptional cases, take a bathroom break to stare at a man with a bad toupee or a woman who misspent a fortune on her platinum helmet. They called the round doorstop a "Betty Ford" in honor of her mastectomy. At 209½ I learned that politeness is not kindness and that wit is not cruelty. If you've been excluded from mainstream rights, you critique the mainstream whatever way you can, especially if you are in good company. The cattiness of gay culture grows from outsider knowledge that eventually makes its way inside, absorbed slowly through both collective and individual permeable skins. Verbal performance is capital in a world where masculinity is defined by physical prowess or by income.

In college, my friend Cathy theorized that we loved gay men because they *wouldn't* have sex with us. They weren't interested in our bodies. "Fag hag" emphasizes the undesired heterosexual woman and the homosexual man, making sex the center. But what if something else were the center? What if attractions and bodies were not categorized crisply? Maybe in another shift of power, the ability to critique the inside while being on the outside was part of our bond.

The first week of freshman year at the University of Virginia, a fraternity invited women in my dorm to a party. I was relegated to the back of the pickup truck they used to transport us. In the grand antebellum mansion where the party was held, with its wood paneling and scuffed floors, we were offered Kool-Aid laced with grain alcohol and stood awkwardly waiting for boys to talk to us. I'd rather be doing homework, I thought, and walked back to the dorm. Later that year, through the art, theater, and architecture departments, I discovered a queer subculture, mostly men and a few women. Their parties revealed a kaleidoscope of desires and fulfillment. I retrieved my coat out from under two men coupled on a bed. The sight of a woman, pressing one hand on a doorframe and the other on another woman's back, drawing her in as they kissed, burned into my memory like a brand.

At 209½ I allowed my subconscious desires to percolate to consciousness, in part by talking about them. I only had sex with Tyrone, but I wanted to have sex with a significant portion of the population—male, female, gay, straight. I was pansexual in desire, if not practice. Under the wet sand of my good-girl persona, yearnings were buried like mollusks, leaving small air holes in the surface, evidence of life.

Don, a tall blond boy from Ohio, lied about having restaurant experience, but Jim and I liked him so much we covered for him. He was jaw-dropping handsome, like a William Hurt with curly hair, but he didn't act as if he knew it. There was something fragile about Don. He gave money to the homeless woman, dubbed Miss Mary, who pushed her shopping cart along Pennsylvania Avenue. His father was an alcoholic who couldn't read or write and who wouldn't believe that his son was gay. Don acquired a dildo collection from a job in a sex shop back home, and on his drive to DC he threw them out the window, one by one, planting phallic trees along the highway to mark his journey into a new life.

Don was a connoisseur of bodies: "He's a swimmer," he'd say. "See that layer of fat over the muscle?" Or, "A soccer player, look at those quads." Don also had business acumen, a combination of sniffing out opportunity and tolerating risk. On weekend mornings, he sold Rosewood pottery and other antiques he brought back from Ohio at DC's open-air markets. Later he would have a restaurant of his own as well as a flower shop and a jewelry studio featuring chain-mail jock straps and colored titanium pins in geometric shapes. He made my wedding ring, a rose gold twist.

From Don I learned details of gay men's sex: bathhouses, orgies (in- and out-of-doors), glory holes, and "the beach," a grassy part of Rock Creek Park near P Street. He didn't make me feel prurient for asking. My friends were like French libertines: consensual *anything* is okay. It would be another two years before the HIV virus was identified and in the news, and fifteen years before the first protease-inhibitor drugs were developed. In 1980, no one I knew was aware of this new virus and the horror it would bring.

One Saturday afternoon before Halloween, I walked into the restaurant, opened the kitchen door, and found Danny, the cold station cook, peeling cucumbers while dressed in a nun's habit. Fresh vegetal mist filled the air. Petite, fair, and delicate in his wire-rimmed glasses, Danny was a founder of the DC chapter of the Sisters of Perpetual Indulgence. On his way to work, he said, he passed two women who did a double-take on seeing him. "Real nuns," he surmised, because often the only evidence that one is a nun—not just a dowdy academic—is a gold cross around the neck.

"Wow," I said. "You make a *great* nun." Danny's habit featured a wimple, a headpiece that focused attention to his heart-shaped face, and floor-length black robes with a woolen belt and turned-back sleeves. He wore rubber-soled oxfords, plus the gold cross. Were it not for the overkill, he could pass. "How about a prayer?" I asked.

Danny put down the cucumber and the vegetable peeler, folded his plastic-gloved hands together, and bowed his head. "Heavenly Father, cease not to watch over us when we have attained ecstasy in the arms of a hunky guy. Be a protector of our expenses as we dress ourselves in your honor. Supply what may be wanting to us through shortsightedness or sinful neglect. Make our scallops tender, our chocolate cake light. Guide our waitrons"—he looked up for a second toward me—"that they may become like Jesus, that they may persevere. Amen."

"Amen," I said, giggling.

Tad, a manager with a temper like a gas flame, was also laughing. "Danny boy, you don't know how lucky you are to buy off the rack. My feet"—he paused to stick one out from under his white apron—"are size eleven. Cost a fortune."

Danny smiled coquettishly and picked up the naked cucumber. He waved it at Tad like a magic wand, almost touching him on the shoulder. "Bless you, my child."

The same age as Jason, Tad couldn't be more different as a manager. There was no pretense about him, no defense, and that made him sexy. Without malice, he looked you in the eye and told you to iron your shirt. With warmth, he complimented your hair. His crush on our straight bartender translated into kindness.

In college, I'd learned that queer parties might involve drag, or at least dressing up. On sale, I bought a pair of gloriously impractical beige Italian pigskin boots and wore them as often as possible. In warm weather, I wore the woven plaid ruffled dress I bought in Spain—the one I wore with white leather espadrilles whose ties wrapped around my calves to my foreign service interview two years before. There, three navy-blue suit-clad interviewers asked me, "What's the biggest problem in the United States today?"

"Capitalism," I answered. My knowledge of politics was rudimentary: capitalism and communism are bad, European socialism is good. Despite my fabulous espadrilles, I couldn't articulate the subtleties that might have gotten me the job.

If I hadn't been such a fool, I could have been one of the regular State Department guests dining at 209½. Or I might have been stamping visas in Mongolia. But then I wouldn't have met Tyrone at the Hilton or stood with two funny men discussing women's shoes. *Amor fati,* says the Stoic philosopher Epictetus. Love your fate. Everything in your life is necessary to whom you become, so don't regret your past. I bought a simple, two-piece black dress for when I hosted, which would have been perfect for that State Department interview. I didn't then know the phrase "we're all in drag," or that throughout history, women dressed like men to gain access—to work on sailing ships, cross the prairie safely, or, like transgender musician Billy Tipton, marry other women. Joan of Arc was tried for transvestism, not heresy. Women more frequently dress like men while men rarely dress like women: Why give up the power of being male? When men do cross-dress, their rejection of male power begs us to read their choices like a poem, closely, looking for lapses in verisimilitude. I learned that even small choices can be acts of will and that bodies can speak more powerfully than words.

At one party our straight bartender wore a flesh-colored body suit to become a naked Mrs. Rose, complete with orange-colored wig and girl patch, and gold wine-foil-wrapped fingers. "Welcome to my apartment," he said at the door. His drag was parody; no one would see him as anything other than male. But when you're not sure whether someone is male or female, you might feel threatened because you sense that you're *supposed* to know. A few people—often rich and elite like Anne Lister but also poor like Sylvia Rivera or middle class like Quentin Crisp—have always defied the conventions of gender, although they paid a price. In a photo from that party, Tyrone (an Arab, in a sheet with a headband) and I (a lion, wearing a yellow cotton head I sewed from a kit) look tame compared to a Carmen Miranda behind us in her fishnets and patent-leather stilettos.

The actor Carol Lawrence sashayed into the restaurant wearing high heels and a sparkly royal blue suit. She was *extremely* friendly, which translated into a kind of noblesse oblige. Celebrities raised the temperature in our little culture. We waited on Ted Kennedy (four-martini lunches), Lady Bird Johnson (and her secret service men), Tom Brokaw, George Will, Françoise Gilot and Jonas Salk, Maya Lin (who at nineteen squeezed lemon into the coffee cream to curdle it), Diana Nyad (who brought her own Tupperware containers for leftovers), and Peter, Paul, and Mary. I recognized Anthony Hecht, poetry consultant to the Library of Congress. He dined with his much younger second wife, Helen, and their five-year-old son, so precocious he ordered his filet mignon *saignant.* Helen's cookbooks had a badly composed author snapshot taken by her husband, one that did not do her justice. By contrast, Anthony's own author photo was a side shot of him in French cuffs with gold links, gazing into the distance as if from Mount Parnassus. My feminist hackles rose up. Nobody noticed.

Waiting tables is the art of knowing how to approach a couple who is bickering, a family for whom the food is merely an excuse for a get-together, or a lobbyist who, after receiving the whole artichoke he ordered, indignantly called me back. He pointed to the mess of chewed leaves on his plate, "This artichoke is tough." I could instruct him (in front of his client) how to eat an artichoke, or I could accept the blame. "I'm so sorry," I said. "Let me bring you the fettuccine."

We were quick, picking up verbal and nonverbal cues from one another and from guests. Who needs another drink, *now*? We were more patient with our guests' moods and idiosyncrasies than we would be with those of anyone else. We loved our customers simply for being human, and we tried to make them love being in our hands (*agape* with a dash of *eros*). To do that, we loved one another along with all our snobberies and cutting insights. "Gaydar" exists in part because queer folk pay attention to detail, to the way people conform—or not—to stereotypes, for their own safety in seeking mates. We gossiped like nobody's business. We confirmed suspicions about a White House correspondent's bulimia by following her into the bathroom with its two unisex stalls. Thereafter, when her name was on the reservation list, we signaled by opening our mouths and pointing a finger down our throats.

On Sunday afternoons, when the restaurant was closed for lunch, we played volleyball on the National Mall courts. "Bring your balls," said Jim to the other waitrons and the kitchen staff. We played for fun, and no one cared if I couldn't spike. Tyrone played, too. If his Jamaican background disposed him toward homophobia, getting to know so many gay men changed that. As for me, even though I already spent so many hours a week with my coworkers, I loved being on their team.

Except perhaps during Princess Di's wedding, when Jason used the occasion to anglicize the menu with clotted cream and potted shrimp, and someone brought in a TV and the guys stood around it that Saturday afternoon.

"That dress has ten thousand pearls."

"She took a risk with those bangs."

"My God, look at the carriage."

"Who cares?" I said, setting tables, deliberately uninterested. "She's not very bright. Really, a kindergarten teacher?"

"Oh, honey," said Jim. "She has to be a virgin. A doctor certified her."

I rolled my eyes, but the men were glued to the screen. Maybe they yearned to be virgin princesses. My grumpiness and snobbery might have had something to do with how pretty she was, or with the general notion of monarchy. At least movie stars' fortunes are based on their work. Virginity is a state of inaction, of withholding. Why should it be praised? Could any of us then imagine that the royal marriage would end in divorce, that Charles was already long in love with another woman? Camilla was kept from the press or remained a secret no journalist dared to broach, although Charles gave himself away when asked if he was marrying for love. On the eve of his wedding, he answered, "Whatever love means." In a letter written five years after the royal wedding, he asked, "How could I have got it all so wrong?"

Tyrone made me aware that during this wedding hoopla, Caribbean immigrants were rioting: Bristol, West Yorkshire, and Brixton. Deaths were rare in the UK because neither rioters nor police carried guns, yet inequities in housing and employment were as obvious as billy clubs, and they inflicted much longer-lasting damage. Who could take in the figure of twenty million pounds of taxpayers' money spent on security for the wedding and not consider what else that money might do?

Philia

One spring Saturday, Tyrone and I planned a dinner party. We'd previously moved the autumn-gold refrigerator from our galley kitchen into the large dining room, so that Tyrone could install a clever flip-down work shelf along the kitchen wall. When, at the end of our lease, the landlady told us she wanted the house arranged as it had been, we removed the shelf and replaced the refrigerator. Happily, it covered the spot where we accidentally melted the vinyl flooring with a bag of warm fireplace ashes. It seemed like a gift not to expose our mistake, not to be required to pay for a new floor. The two years Tyrone and I lived in that house were a honeymoon, on our own island. When I fretted over splitting a bill, he shook his head, saying, "Money is not worth worrying about, woman. I'll pay it." When I complained about cleaning, he said, "All you have to do is ask." It was not the same as reading my mind, but I asked, and I received.

At the riverside docks, Tyrone bought a striped bass (which locals call rockfish) caught that morning. He cut potatoes into perfect ovals to be twice cooked, and I zested lemon rind for the mousse. The citrus scent surrounded us like a halo. Maybe my parents would come around, maybe Tyrone and I could live without barred windows, maybe I would find work teaching. One day that winter when I was running for the bus, something in my back snapped. "Surgery," the orthopedist said. I protested, then he shrugged: "Bed rest." I didn't yet know about Pilates or Feldenkrais, but I did figure out that my lack of upper-body strength along with the bad ergonomics of leaning over people to pour coffee from a fifteen-pound pot had caused the injury. I created work-arounds, like walking empty cups to the full coffee pot or asking the guys to pour coffee, but the job was no longer fun. Perhaps I'd also learned what I needed from working at 209½.

The 209½ lemon mousse recipe used uncooked eggs. This was a decade before the first large salmonella outbreak. It was also a decade before Kenneth Love, once an elegant host at 209½, then a florist to DC's elite society, was murdered by a white, nineteen-year-old hustler who stole his gold watches and escaped in his vintage Daimler. Love's death exposed a trail of bounced checks and defaulted loans. Also in that coming decade, Jason's restaurant empire (209½ was the second of many) collapsed. 209½ is now a Korean fast food joint and Jason a real estate agent.

Within the next ten years, AIDS took the lives of five of my friends, four from the restaurant. Jim's bout with polio as a child had weakened his immune system and sped his death, but what of the others? Tall, handsome Don was the first to die, in November 1990, in a Johns Hopkins hospital room heavily marked with red biohazard warnings. I brought him my hardcover copy of *A Boy's Own Story*. I was afraid to hug him. As if chiding a student who hasn't done the homework, his doctor said, "Other patients have fought harder to stay alive." Baptist churches posted marquees: AIDS = GOD'S CURSE ON A HOMOSEXUAL LIFE. Hemophiliac Ryan White, diagnosed with AIDS at age thirteen after a blood transfusion, was expelled from school and then allowed to return after national media covered his story. I lost touch with 209½ cohorts Tad and Danny, heard of their deaths secondhand, and felt pangs of guilt.

In his poem "For the AIDS Dead," Frank Bidart writes, "Without / justice or logic / without sense, you survived. They didn't. / Nothing that they did in bed that you didn't." My friends spent down their savings to be eligible for Medicaid or racked up their charge cards because death erases debts. Their bodies wasted away, an emaciation I had previously seen only in photos.

But that spring night in 1982, eight of us enjoyed rockfish and lemon mousse, sitting on red metal folding chairs around a table created by placing a door on sawhorses. At Garfinckel's, a department store that discriminated against black people (something I intuited and didn't think to do anything about), I bought a tablecloth to cover the door in the splendor of Portuguese damask. I paid for this with my first credit card. Tracing the raised black numbers and the letters of my name on my Amex card, I felt as adult as the people I waited on. I remained a prudent spender, and in two years I saved ten thousand dollars. As with the money I earned in Switzerland, my savings seemed like a passport, although to what, I didn't know.

At our damask-covered table were two other women: Tyrone's cousin, a dentist in DC, and a friend of mine from Hopkins who was attending Georgetown law school. Mentored by writer Edmund White in hopes of becoming the next Amy Tan, she was instead pressured by her family to go back to Hawaii and work in real estate. With our other guests, Russell, Don, Jim, and his partner, we could have been a poster for diversity, but people weren't yet advertising what was later called "inclusion." Jim brought Rubrum lilies arranged in a vase—Stargazers—dramatically spotted hot pink-and-white flowers with an intoxicating sweetness. He thoughtfully snipped the red stamens so that pollen wouldn't stain our clothes and linens or poison our cat.

Of Tyrone's roasted rockfish stuffed with crabmeat, Don said, "This is the best fish I've ever eaten." It was fresh and flaky, served alongside the crisp potatoes. Because the fish and crab were both still so plentiful in eastern waters, we took them for granted. We drank a lot of white wine and lifted our glasses to make toast after toast. To friendship. To food. To family, however that is formed. To whirled peas! Champagne to our real friends and real pain to our sham friends! We savored the creamy lemon mousse.

Toward the end of the evening, a mouse ran around the perimeter of the dining room, and Russell and I screamed. We remained in that dining room on hard metal chairs because the living room was too small for us, we who made our city larger by living and working in it, by the weight of our bodies and the sound of our voices. And if on this night our past selves floated away like steam from a soup pot, our futures were as impenetrable as the metal bars we never removed.

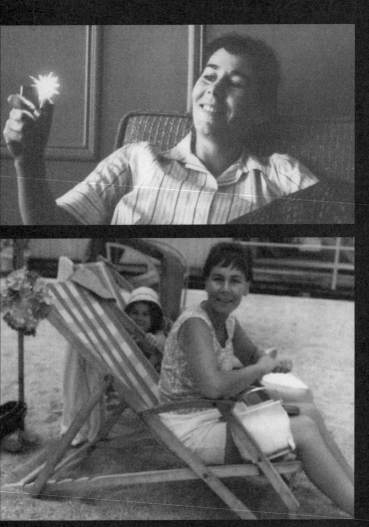

Town of the Big House

BECAUSE I THOUGHT BALTIMORE WAS UNDERGOING A renaissance, I convinced Tyrone to move there from DC. "Baltimore's more real," I said, "and we can afford to buy a house and renovate it." He was eager for a change and happy to please. The neighborhood where we bought our first house had two secondhand bookstores, a coffee shop, a free medical clinic, a feminist bookstore, antique stores, a hardware store (the kind where you can walk in with an odd screw and the clerk will find its mate), the food co-op Sam's Belly, the Butter Crisp bakery, a post office, and an A&P. Three blocks west was the Johns Hopkins campus with its library and swimming pool. When the cat was sick, I put him in his carrier and walked to the vet. Still, the day we moved into that nine-hundred-square-foot house, Tyrone and I were assembling a desk upstairs when someone entered through the unlocked glass-paned front door and stole our wallets from the dining room table.

The name Baltimore comes from the Irish, Baile na Tighe Mor, "town of the big house." Founded in 1729, the city was named after the second Baron Baltimore, Lord Calvert, who held the charter for the Maryland colony. Like a watery hand with hundreds of fingers, the Chesapeake Bay reaches into fertile coastal plain with tall prairie grass as well as forest, once full of elk, bison, wolves, and cougars. Native people were pushed west. African slaves labored for the first Calverts, so from the beginning slaves and colonists were mixed in the complex ways that mark American slavery. Black people could not get married; their families were destroyed. "No pen can give an adequate description of the all-pervading corruption produced by slavery," wrote Harriet Jacobs, once enslaved and later author of a narrative of her years hiding from her master. Although hundreds of slave narratives such as Jacobs's were published in the nineteenth century, as an undergraduate and in an MA program, I didn't read any, because African American scholars or writers weren't hired at the universities I attended, and white professors were mostly not interested.

On my own I read the British Virago imprint: novels by eighteenth-, nineteenth-, and twentieth-century white women that had been popular when published but later were largely forgotten. In my book club, we read "classics" like *Crime and Punishment*. I didn't wonder why neighborhoods east and west of downtown contained decrepit public housing or burnt-out row houses, a legacy, I learned later, of redlining, the fact that black people couldn't buy houses or get mortgages or, when they did manage to do so, only at prohibitive interest rates. I didn't ask why "the highway to nowhere" cut through west Baltimore only to dead-end in a parking lot, and I didn't consider the communities it had displaced. Our own neighborhood was anchored to the north by grand houses built around the green-space vision of landscape architect Frederick Law Olmsted Jr. Like DC, Baltimore was predominantly African American, yet few neighborhoods were integrated. Due to a historical lack of equity in urban development and housing and the absence of black middle and upper classes (unlike in DC), black household wealth in Baltimore was only 5 percent that of white households.

Tyrone's heritage included a seventeenth- or eighteenth-century Scottish master's rape of his African slave. There might also have been a coupling between a Spanish colonist and a Taino or Arawak woman. Caribbean-British Tyrone didn't fully experience the peculiar US legacy of inequality, although of course he experienced a UK version, as well as racism and classism around the world, during his travels. In his early twenties, he discovered a socialist bookstore in Glasgow, Scotland, where his ship was docked. He came back to the ship armed with the writings of Mao Tse-tung, Che Guevara, and Marx and Engels, and after the following voyage, he was not the same person. Awakened to injustice in the world and the idea that it can be ameliorated, he could not forget a dead baby whose skin was coated with feces in a Bombay gutter. He carried that image as he did his chef's knives. When we moved to Baltimore, I had no such image, but I sensed that I needed to learn more. This hunger drove me to earn a PhD in English, a process that instilled in me the notion that the right language could unlock every bright door.

Our second house in Baltimore was one of fifteen unique 1914 Tudor townhouses. They featured herringbone brickwork with half-timbering, steep slate roofs with dormers, oversize chimneys, and multipaned windows. The architect Edward Palmer designed these elegant suburban houses for buyers who didn't need or want a large house and yard. By 1987, of course, Bretton Place was no longer in the suburbs, but the neighborhood remained mostly white. Across the dividing line of Greenmount Avenue, residents were mostly black. Tyrone was the executive chef at one of Baltimore's six Jewish country clubs, and I had four part-time jobs, not including graduate school, so we were rooted, although our social lives were as segregated as the city itself.

Tyrone's friends from work were white, as were mine, from school and the neighborhood. We socialized with two other interracial couples (I'd met the white women through literary circles). I remember wishing I could invite my doctor, a black woman, to dinner. I didn't, because it would transgress a professional boundary. I'd seen a black couple get out of a car in a driveway around the corner about five houses north of ours and asked my elderly neighbor Mary Jane about them. She knew only that the woman was an attorney. I mourned the absence of black neighbors and friends, but I didn't know what to do about it.

The year we bought that second house in Baltimore, also the year I started a PhD program, the price of cocaine smuggled through the Caribbean dropped 80 percent, making the drug widely affordable. Someone figured out how to cook it into little rocks available at only a couple of dollars a rock. Crack provides an instant, brief, but intense high—quickly addictive. White people snorted the white powder, but poor black people were smoking the little rocks. It's satisfying to be able to blame one thing outside ourselves, like a virus or other pathogen, for an illness we suffer from, because then we might get rid of it and feel better. Did cheap crack on top of Baltimore's preexisting conditions of racism and poverty kill the city? Or was crack just a thing that enabled people who didn't use it—like me—to feel clean and healthy?

You entered our house through a boxwood-bordered walk to a side patio with a red quarry-tile floor. Flanked by tall hemlock trees, the patio was cool in summer and shielded from snow in winter. The back garden was framed by another kind of boxwood, faster growing, so thick and tall you couldn't see the alley.

Behind built-in bookcases I found an electric bill from the 1920s and an unopened Christmas card that I replaced for a future owner, along with a dated note, "Natasha and Tyrone love this house and each other." We bought a used shop vacuum in what seemed like a hundred disassembled parts. Even the motor was in pieces. I sat on the couch and studied the instruction booklet. After half an hour, I proudly went to the basement to tell Tyrone that I was ready, but he had not only put it together, he was already using it. It seemed he could solve every problem of living in this house, from knocking down walls to building custom radiator covers.

We scraped wallpaper, a martyrous task I later felt stupid about, when a professional contractor equipped with a steam machine charged only seventy-five dollars to remove wallpaper from the entire three-story stairwell. Under layers in one of the bedrooms, I discovered the wallpaperer's signature with the date May 1914. That first dull pink wallpaper was hung before two world wars, before mustard gas. I planted wild geranium alongside hundreds of tulips, daffodils, and crocus bulbs, and a fragrant white climbing rose from an old five-inch spur given to me by my aunt. Previous owners bequeathed us a quince bush and a peach tree. We enjoyed pride of ownership. The house, even mortgaged with 10 percent interest, framed our middle-class status.

One of my jobs was helping friends who moved to Germany by managing their west Baltimore row houses, bought with credit card down payments as investment properties after being rehabilitated by the city. One house I rented to a white couple in their twenties with two children who were staying with the wife's mother. A friend who owned rental properties advised, "Visit potential renters in their current living space to get a feel for what they're like." The mother's apartment was cluttered but well kept. The man's former employer said, "I think they'll be all right." In a few months, however, neighbors called me to complain about drug-dealing, and I realized that "I think" was code for "no way." The other house I rented to a black, single mother of two children. I visited her apartment too. It sparkled. Her moving boxes were neatly labeled and taped. Her references used the word "trustworthy." But when after a year I looked at the place, I noticed that water damage from a leaking roof had ruined one interior wall. "Why didn't you tell me?" I asked. "I was afraid you'd raise the rent," she said. After evicting the drug dealer, I turned the job over to a management company. I didn't know the language of this rental business, and anyway, it was enough to worry about our own home.

Two years after we moved into Bretton Place, men broke down an elderly neighbor's door, tied her up, and stole everything they could sell. A year after that, on Halloween afternoon, we were not home when our house was burglarized. The police caught the burglar and we were promised restitution, but he'd already sold the electronics, the jewelry, and my best wool suit and leather pumps. We scrambled to find photos and receipts. After the deductible, the insurance payment was a couple hundred dollars. The Japanese binoculars Tyrone used

on sea voyages and my great-grandmother's jade pin were ir-
replaceable. By this time Sam's Belly had closed, as had the
hardware store, the bookstores, and the bakery—replaced by
fast food and check-cashing joints. The Greenmount Avenue
neighborhood changed so incrementally that we didn't realize
it; or, more accurately, we realized it only when it was too late
to react with anything but dulled sorrow.

Every year before Mother's Day, someone dug up our lav-
ender, pansies, and even petunias. Two twelve-year-old boys
tried to pull the purse off my shoulder midday in front of the
Superfresh. I flailed and screamed and ran into the store, at
which point the security guard emerged, looking tired. Our
credit cards were stolen out of the mailbox. We found out
only when the credit card company called; the couple who
stole our cards charged five hundred dollars' worth of clothes.
We cut a mail slot in the door and chained the barbeque to
the back porch. My car was stolen. After it accrued six weeks
of residential parking tickets from the neighborhood where
the thieves left it, I was called to pay a fee and retrieve it from
the pound. A friend held up at gunpoint moved to Oregon.
Returning home from the library after dusk, I strode briskly
in the middle of the street, listening for a rustle behind me,
carrying keys between my fingers, ready to poke them into a
mugger's eyes. I used to walk the three miles downtown, but
the intersection of North Avenue and Charles Street was now
so dangerous I didn't dare. To avoid carjacking, I took the
highway that cut through black neighborhoods.

Tyrone knew that Che Guevara (who had been a caddie in
Argentina) and Fidel Castro considered golf bourgeois, but
he learned the game and took pride in his skill. After one

tournament, Tyrone was given a mug on which had been printed a photo of him and three white men leaning on their clubs. To properly expose the white skin, the camera made Tyrone so dark you can't see his features. Although he usually expressed no dismay at being the only black man, that didn't mean he didn't realize that the color of his skin might affect how people treated him, and us.

On our way back to Baltimore from the beach one sunny afternoon, my bare feet were on the dashboard while Tyrone drove the Mercedes we bought from my father in the left lane. The air-conditioning was on. In my peripheral vision, I noticed a car keeping pace, to my right. It was a two-, some-times three-lane parkway. I glanced over to see who was driv-ing the car: a black woman. Waiting for the exact moment when I looked at her so she could mouth, "Fuck you," give me the finger, and then speed on ahead. What did she see? An average-looking white woman in an indecorous posture next to a black man driving an expensive new car. Perhaps she also saw the internalized racism that prefers whiteness. We both knew her gesture was harmless, but Tyrone put a hand on my thigh. "Don't fret, Pain," he said. "Pain" was one of his nicknames for me, as in "pain in the neck" or "pain in the butt." I had only an inkling of the limits to the gender solidarity between white and black women. As Audre Lorde wrote, "Some problems we share as women, some we do not. You fear your children will grow up to join the patriarchy and testify against you; we fear our children will be dragged from a car and shot down in the street, and you will turn your backs on the reason they are dying."

I might remember the incident in the car because there were so few other times I noticed someone noting the difference in Tyrone's and my skin color. A white guy jumped out of a bar in New Orleans to spit at us. A black man on a Baltimore street muttered, "cookies and cream, yum." More troubling were the things that didn't happen, an absence difficult to pin down. A French professor friend referred to a woman as *insortable*, meaning she couldn't be taken anywhere. Even though the woman was not me, I wondered if the professor might say the same thing about Tyrone. She only invited me over when Tyrone was working. How do I know we weren't invited together—because Tyrone was a chef who worked on weekends or because he was black? I couldn't know, and not just in this friend's case. The unknowable simmered below every surface, creating heat that would not dissipate.

Jamaica Kincaid, who grew up in Antigua, writes: "Race is not particularly interesting to me. Power is. Who has power and who doesn't. Slavery interests me because it's an incredible violation that has not stopped. It's necessary to talk about that. Race is a diversion." By focusing on skin color, we sometimes ignore all the other factors in someone's life—for example, whether they had parents who valued education, or whether they even knew their parents or were raised by someone who loved them.

Another of my jobs was as a poet-in-the-schools, teaching fourth- and fifth-graders. I loved this work, in which children raised their hands before I'd even asked a question. Some squirmed in their seats while others studied me with the concentration of diamond cutters. I liked the ways they revealed their individual personalities in the messiness or neatness of their desks, in the way they made tasks their own.

Teachers tended to prefer docile and conventional students who colored within the lines, who repeated what the teacher said. I tried to recognize the word artists. One student came up with "Madonna is a convertible because she takes her top off." Another wrote, "My father is like a toilet because he stinks when he's drunk."

Linguists George Lakoff and Mark Johnson have shown that metaphor is anchored in concepts central to thinking. For example, the concept "life is a journey" manifests in such expressions as "a good start," "going far," and "being without direction." We use information about one subject to provide understanding of another. Teaching metaphor is standard for poets-in-the-schools; it's fun and the students grasp it quickly.

I asked the Arts Council for posts on Maryland's Eastern Shore, with its placid waterways and verdant farms, when my own academic year was over. I spent a June week in glossy Easton, housed in the guest apartment of a riverfront estate, home to a family who loved modern art. I spent another week in Chestertown, a colonial port where the bed and breakfast was a restored nineteenth-century mansion. The Eastern Shore, separated from Washington and Baltimore by the Bay Bridge, seems bucolic—if you don't look at the chicken farms and trailers where workers, mostly black people, live. "Maryland is below the Mason-Dixon Line," someone said to me, as if to explain its racial divide.

I also spent one week at an elementary school in the George B. Murphy Homes project, the fourteen-story high-rise buildings on Martin Luther King Jr. Highway. The 1961 complex, a short walk from downtown, was named after a founder of Baltimore's African American newspaper. From

a distance, each building looked like it could have been designed by the Swiss architect Le Corbusier. He advocated for
efficient "radiant cities" of high-rise buildings with plazas
and parks and shared amenities that reduce cost.

Baltimore slums without plumbing or electricity were replaced with the George B. Murphy Homes, four high-den-
sity buildings containing 757 apartments. The absence of
trees made the site feel stark, otherworldly. "Architecture is
the will of an epoch translated into space," wrote modernist
Mies van der Rohe. The apartment buildings could have been
warehouses. Balconies were encased in wire, perhaps to prevent children from falling, but in places the wire was bent
or missing altogether. Chunks of concrete from balconies littered the ground, along with garbage and broken glass.

In the heart of Murphy Homes was the George Street
school, cinder block, like many other schools, with wire-
screened windows. Inside, it could have been a school anywhere, with clean, dark-green linoleum floors and wooden
desks. The undecorated hallways—no art projects—had a
sickly cast from the fluorescent lighting, and there was a security guard stationed at the door.

On the first day, I asked my first class of fifth-graders,
"What information am I giving you if I tell you the sun is an
orange?"

Someone said, "It's orange."

"Yes, the color. What else?"

"Round."

"Yes, the shape. So instead of saying 'the sun is round and
orange-colored,' I can just say 'the sun is an orange' and you'll
be able to picture it." I moved to the board, chalk in hand, and
said, "Let's list some animals."

"Dogs!" shouted a boy.

"That's great," I said, writing "DOG" on the board. "What else?"

They were silent. Finally, one student said, tentatively, "Rats?"

"Yes," I said. "Rats are animals. What others?"

After what seemed like several more silent minutes, I coaxed, "Oh, come on, you know lots of other animals." No response. "Animals you've read about or animals you've seen at the zoo?"

The Baltimore Zoo was just over two miles away. "Any of you been to the zoo?"

No one spoke or raised their hand. The teacher interjected, "I don't think so."

I was about to say, "What about cats?" when I realized that none of these children had pets. This stunned me into silence. My mouth probably hung open as I tried to figure out what to do next. Eventually I managed to revise my lesson plan into one where we made metaphors from the school building itself. The floor is the ground. The ceiling is the sky. This wasn't as much fun as animal metaphors, in part because animals make sounds that kids love to imitate. "Hoot, hoot," goes the owl, and what does that sound remind you of?

Fifth-graders especially love being asked to make noises because they're at an age where they're supposed to be past such childish behavior. In any case, I eventually realized these kids could teach me the nouns and sounds of their world, but I was afraid of patronizing them and of leading them into greater darkness. Are skyscrapers like hypodermic needles? What are gunshots like? Part of me assumed I knew.

One boy, chubby and shy, looked at me as if yearning to be called on. I did. When the children were writing their own poems, I went to him and praised his writer's ability to notice detail. I wondered if he'd ever have the chance to practice the craft. What were the chances of him graduating high school, of going on to college? Recently, a colleague explained her academic success despite an impoverished childhood with a single mother: "It was luck, pure luck, that I didn't do drugs or get pregnant."

The George Street students weren't dressed in rags, and they didn't look like they were starving—my historical images of poverty—but it dawned on me that I could not assume anything about their lives. I didn't know if their family members had been to the zoo. I didn't know whom they lived with or how. I didn't know—then—that 90 percent of project residents were unemployed. Sociologist James Coleman's extensive 1966 study of children's school success had by then trickled into common knowledge. He was one of the first to document the gap in achievement between African American and white students. He found that families are the most important factor for success, along with a diverse socioeconomic mix in the classroom. How much teachers are paid is also an indicator of a good educational system; in Switzerland teachers are paid as much as doctors. Baltimore teachers earned more than garbage truck drivers, but only 25 percent more.

Like other fifth-graders, the George Street kids assumed that everyone who publishes a book makes a lot of money from it. But these students saw books only at school. During a break, a teacher took me aside and said, "Some of these kids have never eaten with a fork." If they had a parent, she was likely a single mother and might be addicted to crack cocaine. Prostitution was a way to supply her habit. Getting drugs and avoiding gangs and their violence were her full-time job. Writer D. Watkins, who grew up in Baltimore and still lives there, recalls, "Everybody's parents were junkies, and all the kids were selling or using, and it was like a super escape. So it was an escape for the person that was, you know, putting it into their body, and then it was an escape for a person who was selling it and making money off of them." In fifth grade, the kids probably weren't using drugs yet, but they might be helping to sell them.

During a lesson, two girls started arguing, and before I realized what was happening, they were pummeling each other on the floor. The teacher calmly said, "Darnell, Andre, you know what to do." Each boy took a girl by the arms, pulling her off the other. Pinning the girls' arms behind their backs, the boys marched them to the principal's office. In my own rarified reality, my friends' children went to private schools where being caught writing "slut" on a bathroom stall sent the writer to the principal's office. At George Street, the toilet stalls and even the bathrooms themselves didn't have doors. Graffiti was the least of George Street's troubles.

Some might say that kids with hard lives need foremost to express themselves, to tell others what they are feeling. While that is surely important, the week at George Street made me believe that giving children new experiences is even more important. If you've never seen an orange, you can't compare it to the sun. Life is a journey, but climbing fourteen flights of stairs because the elevator is broken is an exhausting and demoralizing path. It didn't occur to me to figure out a way to take them to the zoo. Or give them a ride on a train, a walk along the river, a meal in a restaurant. Still, my heart ached for the possibilities closed off in the lives of these ten-year-olds. I felt guilty about what I'd been given access to and stymied by how I might share it. Did I think I could change their lives by spending a week teaching metaphor? No. I was there for the money and the experience. If I became weary thinking about the immensity of the problems, I was awed by the perseverance of the schoolteachers and administrators despite their own exhaustion. And although I wanted to climb to the roof of a high-rise and throw chunks of concrete at the inspector or whoever signed papers allowing the complex to be built, I also knew that this neighborhood was part of what I called home.

When we compare one thing to another we erase differences, or rather we focus only on what we want to see. Saying the sun is an orange ignores its incredible heat. When we focus only on one marker of identity, we neglect the complexity of human experience. In his diary, Franz Kafka wrote, "What have I in common with the Jews? I have hardly anything in common with myself." I was relieved to walk out of the George Street school, get into my car, and drive a few miles east to tree-lined Bretton Place. A school in the projects is like one fresh spot in a bad peach. A city turns into a wasp's nest when only some bees can make honey.

Language didn't just fail me while teaching fifth-graders, it also failed me at home. One evening, I returned from teaching to find Tyrone in front of the TV, celebrating OJ Simpson's acquittal with a beer. Sternly, I interrupted his happy glow. "Why are you glad that he will not be prosecuted for murder?"

"It's the system. It's not just OJ, it's the whole fucking system rigged against black men," Tyrone said.

"So to fix the system you let someone get away with murder?"

"Hey, baby, that detective bragged about making up charges. The evidence was rigged."

"But you agree OJ killed Nicole, right?"

"I don't know about that. How can I know? All I know is what the trial brought out."

"I can't believe you're saying that." It was as though we lived on different planets.

Ungently, I shut the door and went to my study, where I was finishing a dissertation on the coquette figure in eighteenth- and nineteenth-century novels. The topic might seem utterly removed from George Street, but I found a connection, the fact that novelists replicate the conventions of their culture even if they rebel against those conventions in their own lives. Coquettes are women who manipulate others with verbal and body language. In another era, or with luck, they might be writers. In English novels, coquettes are disciplined by marriage; in American fiction, they are punished by death, like Edith Wharton's Lily Bart. Yet some female authors like Wharton lived rich and independent lives. Being born female does not exempt you from promulgating patriarchy. Having awareness of one kind of prejudice does not automatically sensitize you to another. Susan B. Anthony argued against the Fifteenth Amendment (which gave black men the right to vote), aghast at the "insult" of putting "every shade and type of manhood over [women's] heads." Tyrone kept race and class in his sights while I was blinded by my feminism.

Later, when Nicole Brown's and Ron Goldman's families won a civil suit against OJ, I asked Tyrone, "What do you think of that?"

"It's a completely different case," he said. "You're ignoring the difference between a civil and a criminal case. The standard of proof is lower in civil cases." I saw everything in broad strokes or looked only at a tiny detail. Putting the two skills together is my devil of a job in life, along with practicing patience. The challenge is not just knowing facts, and it's not just thinking; it's being able to think about facts in a constructive way. Building something from them.

Halfway through our time at Bretton Place, Tyrone's father died. Tyrone said, "I need to tell you something," and five days later his son, Adrian, arrived, sent by his grandmother in Jamaica. I had known about Adrian since the beginning of Tyrone's and my relationship, but I never imagined I would have to live with him. Our house had plenty of room, but I wasn't expecting to share the space. I was not flexible. I was the kind of stepmother who expects a fifteen-year-old boy to be clean, quiet, honest, and hardworking, and when he was not, I harangued, stamped my feet, and pushed him, this teenager who was already much larger than I was. I told myself I didn't know how to talk to him. Adrian retreated into the silence of which his father was a master. Tyrone was the kind of father who alternately jokes with and yells at his son, the kind of father who, when he realizes that these methods won't work, starts drinking more, burrowing into his sadness. I signed us up for family counseling, but I was the only one who went, to two sessions. "The one thing you must not do," said the counselor, pausing for emphasis, "is force Tyrone to choose between you and his son."

Tyrone had visited Adrian only a few times after he brought him to his parents' house in Kingston, and I never even talked to him. Most parents put their children's needs ahead of their own because they love them. Tyrone and I kept working, maybe with even more zeal, using work as an excuse to not engage with the boy living with us. I did things that I thought were important, but they were really attempts to make Adrian conform to my notion of what he should be. I arranged for tutoring so that he could test into Baltimore's best city schools, but he wasn't bookish like me or industrious like his father, and we didn't try to figure out his talents and create opportunities for him to thrive using them. We allowed Adrian in our home, but not into our hearts.

After not quite a year, during which time I learned to anticipate Adrian's musky presence before I turned my key in the door and then sucked in a deep preparatory breath, I was so miserable I said to Tyrone, "I'm going to rent an apartment and live in it and you and Adrian can live here." Instead, Tyrone sent Adrian to his cousin's household in Brooklyn. The cousin had two children around Adrian's age and was renovating a brownstone in Bedford-Stuyvesant. Adrian's cousins were good kids who didn't do drugs, who went to school. Tyrone chose me over his son, evidence of how closely we were bound, of how much he loved me. I told myself Tyrone made the choice, even that he was relieved to make it. I tried to stop thinking about how we might have resolved our problems without Adrian moving out. Our household became a microcosm of the city itself: irreparably damaged by inequity. It fell on us, the adults, to adapt, but we did not and we didn't even admit our failings. Gaston Bachelard comments that the thresholds of domestic space, the windows and doors, let us see both inside and outside and thus blur boundaries in ways that can be subversive. Our house had seven exterior doors, forty-six windows, and four porches. If the outside was a city—a world—where racism and violence reigned, what was the inside of that beautiful house? Not a sanctuary and not a place of integration, but a space in which we used our hands to renovate floors and walls, and also to turn out our child.

A psychologist I was seeing asked me to draw a tree and a house. I drew a leafy apple tree full of round apples, and a house with many windows and a prominent front door. I knew the healthy optimism I was representing, that I should not draw a bare-branched tree in winter or a house without openings. Yet I was performing an optimism I did not feel. Bachelard notes about the world of the spirit, "If one were to give an account of all the doors one has closed and opened, of all the doors one would like to re-open, one would have to tell the story of one's entire life." In reopening the doors to Bretton Place, I reenter a state that I had tricked myself into forgetting.

In summer the green of a horse chestnut tree shaded my study. I loved looking out the window in between the lines or sentences I was writing. But that tree was dying, I could tell from its increasingly shortened seasons and lack of fruit, the papery sound of leaves under my shoes in August. It had been done in by disease—bleeding canker, leaf blotch, fungi, scale, or leaf miner—or pollution, or both. Horse chestnuts *can* be long-lived. The tree that Anne Frank looked upon lasted more than 150 years. "Nearly every morning I go to the attic to blow the stuffy air out of my lungs. From my favorite spot on the floor I look up at the blue sky and the bare chestnut tree, on whose branches little raindrops shine, appearing like silver, and at the seagulls and other birds as they glide on the wind. As long as this exists, I thought, and I may live to see it, this sunshine, the cloudless skies, while this lasts I cannot be unhappy," she wrote. When a Bretton Place tree died, the city eventually replaced it with an eight-foot sapling. It was incongruous to have a fifty-foot tree next to a sapling, but it was hopeful.

On a few acres in Lancaster County, Pennsylvania, along with other fruit trees, my father grew edible chestnuts. He pretended that he never rejected his good-natured and forgiving son-in-law. Years later, however, when I had a Fulbright in Slovenia, my cousins were surprised when I told them my husband would visit. "Your father told us you were single," one cousin said. My father thought his honor was destroyed when his only child married a black man, even though that black man helped him prune his trees, took him fishing, and repaired his tractor. When I came back from Slovenia, I asked my then eighty-nine-year-old father, "Why didn't you tell the family about Tyrone?" He refused to answer.

In Baltimore, my father gave us a bag of chestnuts. I planned to candy them. I left the bag on our new Formica counter and went to bed, dreaming of the sweet nuggets. The next morning I saw hundreds of white worms the size of an eyelash crawling over the counters. The chestnuts didn't appear to have holes. I considered cooking them anyway, thinking maybe all the larvae left. Or that they didn't matter; canned creamed corn contains a good percentage of worms,

I'd read. But the chestnuts were so small, it seemed like a lot of work to peel them if they wouldn't finally be edible. I threw them in the compost and for a few days continued to wipe up weevils. Perhaps it was my relationship—or lack thereof— with my father I was throwing in the compost. Where it could turn into something else, something eventually more nourishing. Perhaps I can't forgive my father because I can't forgive myself for not loving Adrian.

Tyrone and I bought the Bretton Place house for $100,000 and sold it thirteen years later for $133,000, having spent nearly $30,000 in materials and $3,000 a year in taxes. A house may be "an instrument with which to confront the cosmos," as Bachelard says, but it is not an investment, because inflation-corrected prices of houses remained the same during the years 1890 to 1990, and even later than that in some areas. Still, in the United States, owning a house is central to the middle-class dream.

A few years before we left Baltimore, civil rights groups sued the Department of Housing and Urban Development for segregating public housing and for moving the poorest African Americans into black neighborhoods that were already poor. The George Street high-rises were dynamited in 1999, the year after we left, replaced by a mix of rental and owner-occupied row houses named "Heritage Crossing." The name reflects the neighborhood's long evolution, crossing from slum to slum to working and middle class. The school was torn down, too. I don't know if any of those fifth-graders remember the metaphor lesson. Or how many are alive. When I think about them, I think about my complicity in their fate. I walled myself off from them, maybe not as much as some people, but certainly more than others. I think also of the fact that I walled myself off from Adrian. I was worse than the birth mother who abandoned him because I pretended to be better.

When I was offered a full-time job in Salt Lake City and we were about to move, Adrian said, "You're going to miss this house." By this time, he'd replaced his Jamaican accent with one from New York City. He was twenty-one, attending community college, with a job taking care of troubled teens. Clearly, he had a gift for managing difficult people.

"Yes," I said, recalling the stencils I painted and the boxwoods I watered in the middle of the night during a drought. Our aged neighbors, Dr. Sam and nurse Mary Jane Morrison, who diagnosed my sinus infection and whose walk we shoveled. The parties we hosted in the wainscoted dining room. The study where I wrote so many words and then deleted most of them...

But not the city, I thought. Baltimore taught me that some dreams will not be fulfilled in my lifetime, no matter how hard we work or try. That language is all we have. That work must be its own reward. That personal failures multiply too easily into social ones. That individuals can change but institutions change too slowly. That promises go sour and there's nothing to do but apologize and move on. That we can't lock ourselves into a house, even one with so many windows and doors. Perhaps especially one with so many windows and doors.

Guilt:
A Love Story

The mind is its own place, and in itself /
Can make a Heav'n of Hell, a Hell of Heav'n.

—MILTON, *PARADISE LOST*

AS I ENTER FROM THE PARKING GARAGE, MY SANDALS squeak on the shiny marble floor, the colors of a tiger's eye gem. That and the rich wood paneling belie the fact that this is a hospital. But across from the elevator is a desk with hand sanitizers, masks, and tissues under a sign ("Help Us Avoid the Flu") and a rack of pamphlets ("Coping with Cancer," "Eating Well When You're Not Well," "For Families and Friends"). None of this is new to me. I'm visiting my friend Rand, who has an aggressive leukemia. I know the fourth floor well because Tyrone stayed there often during his treatment for lymphoma.

When I get to Rand's room with its view of the rocky hillside, he's propped up in bed reading a newspaper. An IV line from the unit next to the bed pumps a clear liquid into a vein in his arm. This is his first hospitalization, so he doesn't have a port for his chemotherapy. He smiles broadly and readjusts his body to allow me to lean over to hug him. Then I sit on a chair next to the bed, my feet resting on the rail. He asks, "Does this place bring back bad memories?"

"Not at all," I say. "When I was last here, Tyrone was alive."

Then guilt washes over me.

A "Test of Self-Conscious Affect" asks the reader to imagine killing an animal while driving. How likely you are to react in each of these ways?

A. The animal shouldn't have been on the road.
B. I'm terrible.
C. "Well, it's an accident."
D. I should have been more alert driving down the road.

My answer is D. Isn't everyone's?

Response A indicates externalization, B indicates shame, C indicates detachment, and D indicates guilt, a response to a mistake.

The novelist Roberto Calasso writes, "The primordial crime is the action that makes something in existence disappear: the act of eating. Guilt is thus obligatory and inextinguishable. And given that men cannot survive without eating, guilt is woven into their physiology and forever renews itself." I imagine cave dwellers eating their hoard of gathered berries and dead animals, and wonder if the stronger ate as much as they wanted, the weaker got what's left. Perhaps Calasso is right. San tribal hunters in the Kalahari desert stay with a felled animal until it dies, sharing in its death pangs. But is this guilt or gratitude? Or just practicality, so that the disabled animal is not devoured by a predator?

There is such a thing as "Jewish guilt." And "Catholic guilt." The rule-bound religions of Judaism, Christianity, and Islam focus on sin. Conversely, "the Egyptians, Babylonians, Greeks, and Romans had no word in their language for sin; the Israelites introduced both the word and the concept into the stream of Western civilization, and by so doing, diverted it," writes Leonard Shlain. Instead of consigning human destiny to fate, these religions gave individuals the power of free will—as well as the power to sin. Perhaps this shift also contributed to the idea of an individual self, a concept that seems natural to us now.

My father took me to a Catholic church once or twice at Easter or Christmas; from the mass I retained nothing except a feeling of boredom. So I can't blame Catholicism for my heavy sense of responsibility.

But I can blame my mother.

The first time I saw a therapist I was thirty-six years old. In her office with its subdued light, deep blue walls hung with abstract paintings, and cushioned armchairs, we talked about what I wanted to accomplish. Then I glanced at my watch. I said, "Well, it's been an hour. I should go."

She looked at me quizzically. "Was your mother depressed when you were a child?"

"Yes," I said, astonished that I could have betrayed us so easily.

Neither my father nor I could ever give my mother what she needed—the security of her own mother, whom she lost at age two. Born in 1929 in Breslau, Germany, my mother's life was disrupted by war; she didn't have the luxury of therapy. The only brown-haired, brown-eyed one in the family, she was told, "The gypsies left you on the doorstep." She became a person unable to ask for what she wanted, afraid to displease or risk rejection. When my parents were first married, she was so timid she asked my father's permission to go to the movies, and when he mindlessly said no, she stayed home. She thought being loved depended on her obedience, as with her own father. Even with me, she was timid. Why couldn't she just say she wanted ice cream, instead of asking me if I wanted some and then denying her own desire when I didn't? I felt like the mother, the one in control.

Now I wake up thinking, *I should visit her,* which I do twice a week. She lives only a mile away in a senior apartment. I imagine her next to me in the passenger seat, waving her hand in front of my eyes to point out mountain vistas. On days I don't visit her, I fall asleep to the dirge, *tomorrow.*

Because of Alzheimer's and her lack of ability to smell, and aphasia, my mother makes a face when she tastes foods she formerly loved: crab cakes, asparagus with hollandaise, endive salad. Sweetness is her only remaining delectation. She eats handfuls of Dots and mini 3 Musketeers, candy she once scorned. Anxiety exacerbates her symptoms, so I try to spare her anything that might cause it, except my own recognition of her failing. Which I can't hide. Which makes me feel even guiltier. My recognition of her disease and its symptoms is an irrational way of protecting myself—as if hyperawareness were a vaccine. The tangles and amyloid plaque in the brain blossom: orange thistles growing amid the trumpet vines. The tau proteins disintegrate from within their proper places in the neurons like tiny firecrackers.

I sense what she wants from me—love and acceptance— and I feel guilty that I limit the former and cannot give the latter. Why do I correct her when she picks up a piece of garbage from the ground? I also feel guilty wondering when she will die, hoping that it will be before too long. Before she loses language altogether. Before she must be fed. I try not to think about how nice it would be to add her savings to my own.

Feeling responsible for my mother and her happiness—and by extension everyone else I care about—is an awkward package I drag around. As I write this, I am trying to open it.

Research shows that women feel guilt more than men do. Probably because of the pressure of social forces: women are expected to do more for others and to bear more responsibility. Yet people who feel guilty are infantilized, subject to a higher authority. I feel responsible for my mother's inability to seize her own happiness, perhaps because I witnessed it my whole life.

Or perhaps because I learned to seize my own happiness. Like my father. Our crime: self-interest instead of tenderness. The expression "guilty pleasure" suggests eating chocolate or reading trashy magazines, something unhealthy or unedifying. The root of my guilt and my pleasure is not just that I fell in love with someone else so soon after Tyrone's death, but that I primed myself to do so. How? By imagining a life without him while he was still alive. By knowing he would die and, during his illness, by preparing myself for his death in practical and psychological ways, with the consequence of my not being fully present for him.

Practical: Tyrone had a $100,000 term life insurance policy whose premiums became exponentially more expensive as he passed sixty-five. We had bought this policy when he was supporting us in Baltimore, but after our move to Salt Lake, I was the breadwinner and we didn't need it. Each year when he was ill, I wondered if, by paying the premium, I was placing faith in his death rather than his life. The year he died, I almost didn't pay the $2,700. I wrote one check and shredded it. Then I wrote another and mailed it, not mentioning it to Tyrone. This memory is like a wasp's nest built in the doorframe of my consciousness. Every now and then one of them stings me. Or threatens to, which is worse because it makes me cower.

I loved Tyrone deeply and loyally. I cooked, cleaned, and paid bills. I took him to medical appointments and managed his care, all the while teaching full-time. That work was the hardest I'd ever done. A woman I knew, a massage therapist, stopped me on the street. "I don't usually offer free massages to people," she said. "But you look like you need one." I was too busy to take her up on it.

While Tyrone was at home recovering from his second round of chemo after his first relapse, I lay in the twin bed next to my father, stroking his comatose forehead until he died. My exhausted mother slept in the guest room. But are duty and diligence the point? An irrational part of me believes that I did not love Tyrone enough, otherwise he'd still be alive.

How can I know what "enough" is? This strikes me as love's central question. Love is bottomless, unfathomable, immeasurable. At least that's what romance tells us. "There is no love in heaven," a friend who lost his wife to cancer told me. "That's why we must love on earth." He made his dying wife's care his sole focus, and he is guilt-free. He quotes e. e. cummings's "love is more thicker than forget": "it is most sane and sunly / and more it cannot die / than all the sky which only / is higher than the sky." Perhaps his lack of guilt is simply the difference between his character and mine.

If Tyrone were alive, we would be settled further into the monotony and comfort of the long-married, vacationing in warm places. On our last trip together, to Jamaica, before the cancer came back, before the stem cell donors reneged, before we were told the only care left was palliative, we drove around the edges of Cockpit Country, a landscape of hills and hollows and very few roads, populated by Maroons, descendants of escaped slaves. *Difficult country,* the guidebook warned, referring not only to the landscape but also to the fiercely enforced isolation of those who live there.

The last hurricane two years before had toppled all the street signs. To find out where we were, we'd slow the car near any person on the roadside, roll down the window, and yell the name of the town next en route to our destination, which I knew from looking at the map. I learned not to yell the destination itself; we'd be met by blank stares, as country people had no idea how to get beyond a twenty-mile radius. This strikes me as a trope for Tyrone's illness. I knew the destination—death—but we only talked about the next town, one in which there was still hope.

Milk River, Jamaica, is an old spa haunted by ghosts. In the eighteenth century, a slave was severely beaten for stealing some cakes. He escaped from the dungeon, ran away, and discovered a mineral spring. He healed his wounds by bathing in it. Then he returned to his master, and in exchange for mercy, he revealed the location of the miraculous spring, fifty times more active and potent than the Vichy water of France.

Tyrone and I were the only guests of the Milk River Spa, which was last renovated in the 1940s. In the dining room, we sat on red Naugahyde-covered heavy wooden chairs. The tables were covered with slick flower-printed oilcloth. The porch, windowed on three sides, let in soft tropical light. The elderly waiter was used to being alone, and a tinny radio blasted his favorite station over the sound of a rotating fan. Tyrone recognized the music as mento, related to calypso, a traditional style of music that preceded reggae.

After a lunch of steamed shrimp and stewed goat, Tyrone and I soaked in the hot mineral water, rich in magnesium, calcium, sulfate, and natural chloride, and so radioactive we were advised not to stay longer than half an hour in our shared tank.

Leaning against the blue tile wall and submerged to his chest, Tyrone said, "It wouldn't take much to revive this place. It has everything. Ocean, healing spring, cheap land. With the spring right here and the ocean a mile away, no one needs to go into the river with its crocodiles."

Before lunch we'd walked to the littered beach to swim. We were the only tourists. People fished and bathed in the ocean. Some even lived on the beach in shacks they'd built out of scrap metal and wood. We'd gotten lots of looks, friendly, curious, or hostile. I picked up a chunk of white brain coral, the size of my hand and heavy as stone, that had washed up on the beach. Waves had smoothed the mazelike grooves, once home to a colony of invertebrates, each shorter than an eyelash. I was holding the exoskeleton of hundreds of thousands of these creatures. In the nineteenth century, the coral reefs around Jamaica were so vast that owners of grand houses used coral to build floors and steps.

Tyrone went on. "If only the roads were better. And then there's the problem of materials." We'd driven from Treasure Beach, farther west, and the sixty kilometers had taken two hours, with Tyrone swerving the car to avoid the ruts and hazards. Some roads still hadn't been cleared from the hurricane.

"I know you could manage the renovation," I said. "The structure is good, it's just cosmetic stuff that needs updating," I said, raising myself out of the water that now felt too hot. Jamaicans build houses with concrete and brick, not wood and particle board. In Salt Lake, Tyrone had turned a typewriter shop into a catering kitchen, with an office, a prep area, and room for storage. We had consulted a feng shui expert on the placement of appliances and furniture as well as colors. "Wind-water" is the literal translation of this Chinese art of permitting ch'i, life energy, to flow freely through a space. The kitchen's location at the rear of the building made it cool and quiet, and the many windows created a cross breeze. When you walked into the pale blue front office with Tyrone's diplomas and certificates behind his large desk, you felt he was in charge, and when you stepped foot on one of the many cushy mats in the celery-green kitchen, you wanted to cook. You felt like anything could be made delicious.

Outside in the brilliant sun, we continued our scheme of renovating paradise, with Tyrone's illness a shadow we couldn't acknowledge. At night, tiny mosquitoes the size of gnats swarmed and bit, but the bites were so small they didn't welt.

After Tyrone died, I should have fallen into a depression. Instead I was happy, relieved of the stress that, among other things, had made me lose my hair.

Other things I feel guilty about:

1. Wasting food. As I write this two pounds of grapes I picked from an untended vine are desiccating in the refrigerator. On the vine, they would have been eaten

by birds or rats, but I brought them home and then forgot about them. Or rather, I can't forget about them and I also can't throw them out. I intend to get the food dehydrator and turn the grapes into raisins, but this requires me to pick them off their stems, and that will take a good hour. It will also use two days of electricity to make half a pound of raisins. I am caught between committing a sin from my childhood and the ridiculous waste of energy that avoiding it will entail.

2. Wasting money. Related to wasting food and my immigrant childhood. My grandfather said, "We're too poor to buy cheap things." He told a story of one salted herring hung in the middle of the table while each of the ten children swiped their boiled potatoes against it. I wear a pair of men's 1969 tailored-in–Hong Kong cashmere pants that I bought for twenty-five dollars at Community Thrift and paid another seventy-five dollars to have altered. With care, they will last until I die.

3. Wasting time. "Time is *not* money," I recite to myself like a prayer. Dating from Antiphon, 480–411 BCE, the metaphor of time as currency to be spent is emphasized in US culture. Ben Franklin kept raising the price of a book because he perceived a potential buyer as wasting his time by repeatedly asking for a lower price.

Time is more precious than money because it can't be replaced or earned. "There's not enough of it," Tyrone said in his last weeks, sitting on the loveseat wrapped in a thick bathrobe and wearing a knitted wool hat over his bald head. Perhaps that's why I wasted no time falling in love again.

The winter after Tyrone died, I asked our neighbor for help in fixing the TV reception. He looked at his feet and, after a pause, said his wife knew more than he did about electronics. I had the sudden, uncomfortable, broaching-on-awful realization that he thought I was coming on to him. "Sure," I said, "I'd love it if she could come over and take a look." They both did, although neither could fix the TV.

I had become the widow in need of consolation, some amalgam of footloose and grief-stricken, but I did get a lot of work done in those months after Tyrone's death, which made me realize how much time a relationship takes. When there's no one to cook with or for, when there are no negotiations about when or why or what. When time stretches ahead broken only by one's own decrees. I will eat only cold food today. I will not take the newspaper from the driveway nor bring it inside the house. I will do whatever I want. What is that, exactly? It was easier to come home from my office at the college at ten than at six, easier to throw myself into work that might prove to me that I was still strong and capable.

I worked late at the college because evenings at home I missed Tyrone most. One evening there was a knock at my office door. I opened it, expecting to find a student who needed help with a paper. It was a friend, Laura. She had a gift-wrapped book in her hand, Tess Gallagher's *Moon Crossing Bridge*, poems written after the death of her husband, Raymond Carver. Laura lived in the neighborhood and had stopped by because she'd noticed my light on. I hadn't seen her since the memorial service. "When you're ready," she said, "I'd like to take you out to dinner." Later she said she meant that invitation innocently, that she did not presume my interest in her. But her sentence lodged in my brain like a nugget of gold that I might scratch from when I felt poor. I went home and read the poems and wept. Tyrone's hot pepper sauce was still in the refrigerator, his Tetley tea in the cupboard, his wool sweaters and caps in the closets.

When later that winter I told a friend that I wanted to start dating, she said, "So soon?" She had read that for each year of a relationship a person needs a month of mourning. That meant another two years for me. She wasn't counting the three years that I prepared for Tyrone's death.

During spring break I went to Mazatlán, Mexico, where friends owned a house, and at a carnival party I flirted with a man from Vancouver. To the potluck he had brought ripe tomatoes and basil dressed with a balsamic reduction—the simple act of making the vinegar thicker transformed the dish. Tyrone's gift for cooking had always attracted me, his abilities to meliorate and to give. The Canadian held my hand in his and I felt a wave of hope, of possibility. I gave him my business card and fantasized about trips to the Northwest. When I got home, I trolled match.com and asked friends to "fix me up." On a lark I took the eHarmony test (at that time entirely heterosexual) and, without paying for an online profile, was offered dozens of men. The algorithm found cosmopolitan lawyers and real estate developers, gradually increasing in wealth, not a single chef or artist. What had I answered to prompt that, I wondered? Instead, I contacted a minister whose online match.com profile said he loved poetry and spoke German—whose direct gaze and handsome face had attracted me from the screen. But when the recently divorced minister and I met, neither one of us dipped a toe into the water.

How I pity those who lose their loved one suddenly.

Rand's wife, Rebecca, gives me their community agriculture share for the rest of the season; she's living in Rand's room at the hospital. I did not live in the hospital with Tyrone because—my excuse—we had two cats. Each week I cook vegetables into something I can bring to them. I make curried red lentil soup and minestrone. A pasta salad for Rebecca. Corn cookies for Rand. I use food to express love in part because I am a good cook. Tyrone's and my parties were legendary, at least to our friends. He could make hors d'oeuvres out of daylilies. He could fillet a fish so cleanly the skeleton lifted off like a piece of toast from a plate. He could look at me and know what I was thinking.

Rand is neutropenic, which means his immune system can't handle bacteria or viruses. I remember those periods in Tyrone's life. I use a lot of turmeric, whose antibacterial, antioxidant, and anti-inflammatory qualities are now being recognized in the United States as well as in India. I worry about kitchen hygiene. Sometimes I use the dishcloth to wipe the floor; sometimes I taste the soup with a spoon I've licked.

I regret not spending every minute with Tyrone while he was sick. One month before he died I was upstairs, working furiously on a paper for a conference that a friend and I planned to attend. I worked all evening to beat the midnight submission deadline while Tyrone watched TV alone in the den downstairs. Hearing the laugh track, I wondered if I should go down. I didn't. The conference never happened.

I regret not spending more money on our travel. When he visited me during my Fulbright to Slovenia in 2005, I rented a rent-a-wreck Daewoo without power steering, power windows, or air-conditioning. Tyrone cursed every minute in that car. A BMW passed us on the highway as if we were in a horse-and-buggy, and Tyrone turned to look at me: *Why did you think this was a good idea?* I regret other economies that I practiced over our thirty years together. I knew they irritated him, and I regret them especially because I am left to enjoy the money I saved. With my new love.

An astrologist told me I have a grand trine in water, like a protective moat around my ego. "Three planets in water signs make a triangle in your chart." He made a cone shape with his two hands. "Imagine a tripod balancing on buoys in the ocean—it can't tip." His hands rocked back and forth as if the air were water. The positive aspect is the ability to self-comfort; the negative aspect is the way self-sufficiency alienates others. A water grand trine also indicates psychic awareness. Sometimes I disregard information gained intuitively because I don't want to deal with it. It is easier not to know when someone is jealous of you, for instance. Or when your mother wants you to stay. Yet unspoken desires float like a murky pool under every human transaction. In my long marriage with Tyrone especially, I knew what he wanted from me: sex, respect, and for me to stop nagging.

Someone told me that whatever—absolutely whatever—one feels after the death of a loved one is grief. In trying to understand guilt, I am grieving Tyrone.

In one dream, I am walking alone at dusk when I see him coming toward me, wearing his olive-green insulated jacket and the natural wool cap my mother crocheted to cover his head. He is still somehow substantial and muscled, fueled by the immunosuppressant drug Prednisone that had him whacking the tiles off the downstairs bathroom, exposing the uneven gray cement.

He speaks first. "I want you to be happy."

I say, "Some dying spouses tell their partners to marry again."

Then he drifts away, and something pulls and snaps in my chest like a rubber band.

Psychologists have a theory for how we can understand what someone else feels. Simply observing another person's emotional state can create that state in the observer. This explains the power of film and the power of personal testimony. An empathetic person can feel anticipatory guilt. Perhaps I pretend to be empathetic because it is socially required, an extension of manners. Perhaps I am writing this essay to produce guilt adequate to what I think I should feel. One of the tenets of postmodernism is that pretense is real, an idea supported by neurological research that shows the same areas of the brain activate when someone is pretending sadness or truly sad. Along the same lines, behavioral scientist Paul Dolan argues that behavior changes the brain patterns that change the self. My guilt becomes real as I write it.

Jungian therapist Lawrence Staples believes that creative human beings commit "sins" that benefit them, that they have an "obstinate and irreverent insolence toward authority that is informed by a love of freedom." Staples notes that those who challenge social norms might feel guilty, but like Prometheus's theft of fire, their sins benefit humankind. They change the social order. During our marriage, Tyrone and I changed the social order because he was black and I was

white. Now that I am partnered with a woman, we also challenge the social order. I feel no guilt about either relationship.
If anything, I feel defiant, especially living in a theocratic
state. Perhaps this is just self-preservation. Falling in love
with Laura, who is eleven years younger than I am, means
that now I'm with someone who will probably live longer
than I, who will take care of me when *I'm* sick.

Guilt stimulates different areas of the brain at the same
time. It's considered a more complex emotion than anger,
fear, sadness, joy, or pain. Guilt is a string, sometimes a rope,
tugging at different parts of my brain. Sometimes the line is
slack, sometimes so tight it hurts. It dawns on me that guilt
is part of love. In fact, guilt is the way I learned to express
love.

In another dream, I'm in bed with Laura when I sense that
Tyrone is in the house. I eagerly get up to find him, but I am
also torn and remorseful because I can't be in two beds at the
same time.

The first doctor Tyrone saw for the swelling under his eye,
a Chinese-born ophthalmologist, told him, "A blocked tear
duct. You can wait for me to operate until after Christmas."
Christmas was three months away. Why did we accept that
diagnosis? Why did I not remember that any swelling could
be dangerous? Years before, a worried student stretched
out her swollen hands in front of me as if showing off a
wedding ring. She knew enough to not accept her local
doctor's remedy of steroids and flew to the Mayo Clinic
where her lung cancer was diagnosed and treated. She is
alive today.

Five months after that first visit, after Tyrone's biopsy and lymphoma diagnosis, that doctor sat facing us from behind her imposing desk. "Yours is such an unusual case," she said, as if congratulating herself on finding a research topic. Her framed diplomas covered the wall behind her. "Feng shui," I thought. Much later, she would have her nurse call and ask for his medical records, "to update the file." "No," I would say, and then slam down the phone, trembling with indignation.

In the ophthalmologist's suburban office, light from the wide windows flooded the room. I looked at Tyrone, his eye still bandaged in white. This was the first time I'd accompanied him. He'd chosen this doctor because, back in October, she could see him right away. During the first seven or so years that Tyrone and I lived together, I made his doctor and dentist appointments, and I made sure he kept them. I also tried to keep him from drinking too much. I explained this to myself by saying that I was better organized, that I was American. Gradually, in conversations with friends and through therapy, I recognized that my taking responsibility was unhealthy, for both of us. I stopped calculating how much he'd drunk; I stopped keeping track of his tooth cleanings; I stopped choosing doctors. While part of me felt liberated, another part felt guilty. Wasn't that my role?

I looked at the ophthalmologist's light-struck countenance, resisting the urge to nod, the urge to speak. Would Tyrone's outcome be different if his disease had been diagnosed earlier? Would another ophthalmologist have been more careful?

I left the ophthalmologist's office energized. I would find the best for him, I vowed. Not long after, the only lymphoma specialist in Utah agreed to take Tyrone as a patient. For three years, we saw her once a month, often more. She reminded me of a sparrow, quick and delicate.

Tyrone was infected with the HTLV 1–2 viruses, retroviruses that jumped from animals to humans and, like HIV, agents of many diseases—although at a much lower rate than HIV. More than twenty million people carry HTLV, endemic in southern Japan and the Caribbean, yet only a tiny percentage know they do. Tyrone's oncologist was surprised when he tested positive because the cellular tests showed that his lymphoma was not caused by these viruses. "Unusual," she said, "but ultimately unimportant in the way your disease is treated."

I google her name as I write this. Everyone raves about what a good doctor she is. They are happy to be alive. Seeing the image of her face calls forth a combination of comfort and calm. I think of a poem by Fernando Pessoa's heteronym, Ricardo Reis. It ends, "Put all that you are into the smallest things. / Thus the moon gleams in every pond, / As it rides so high." The sparrow doctor put the whole of her kind and intelligent being into the smallest things.

After the first successful round of chemo, when Tyrone and I gave her a present—a pillow of red flowers needlepointed by my mother—she wanted to refuse it. "I'm superstitious," she said. "I like to wait until the patient is in remission."

In Tyrone's case, therapies hadn't been developed for a lymphoma uncommon in the United States, and an initial round of chemo did not knock out all the lymphoma cells. There weren't any willing stem cell donors. One brother was not a match, one brother had died, and his schizophrenic brother refused to be tested. Two people in the UK were identified as good matches, but both reneged after being asked to donate. Why bother registering if you're not willing to spend two days donating stem cells? Rand's sister did this twice, but then, she loves Rand.

Doctors don't place the animal in the road. Nor do they drive over it. Most of the time. One in four patients who enters a hospital is harmed by what happens to them there, by an infection or a caregiver's error.

I realize that the Chinese ophthalmologist lives in my neighborhood. In fact, Laura and I have been walking past her huge and ugly house on our evening strolls. It has three garages and thirty steps to a plain door too small for the rest of the structure. We know the names of her German pointer dogs, we have met her sons and her husband, have even discussed her sons' college choices with her. Mostly we run into her alone because she is the one who briskly walks the dogs. Early on, she asked, "Are you mother and daughter?" In her world, two women walking together every night would have to be family members. She didn't look at our faces closely enough to realize our age difference is only ten and a half years. She dyes her own gray hair. I didn't tell her we met before. It is a secret I tell Laura and one that I hold in my pocket like a rock I can throw in the future.

"Maybe it's cultural," I say to Laura about the doctor's bluntness, her lack of recognition. "Maybe white women all look the same to her. In China, people ask a lot of questions. Someone told me it's part of the competitive culture." I wonder if I'm being harder on the doctor because she's a woman or an immigrant, who must learn not only medicine but also a whole

other context for it. Or is it her personality that makes her so—
what? Unlikable? A word used to put women in their place.

Then once at the gym, while I'm getting dressed, she comes
in from the sauna and opens the locker next to mine. I say
hello, using her name.

She looks at me in surprise. "I know you," she says. But
she can't recall my name or the fact that I live in her neighborhood. Her lack of recognition might be self-protection.
She has given many patients and spouses bad news, but observing their emotional states has never caused her to mimic
their emotions. At home, I google her and discover that patients rate her "below the national average" in every category.
I'm about to add my opinion when I see the two-year window
for comments.

Another doctor Tyrone and I consulted was an infec-
tious-disease specialist, a researcher originally from Puerto
Rico who didn't see many patients with HTLV in Utah. In
fact, he'd never seen any. "The difference between HIV and
HTLV transmission," he said, turning both hands into fists
and rubbing the knuckles together, "is that the HTLV virus
has a hard time breaking the cell barrier."

"That's why you," he said, nodding toward me, "were able
to stay negative." I register the fact that he is attractive and
that he does not wear a wedding ring. I also notice the grim-
ness of his windowless office.

What *did* trigger Tyrone's lymphoma? The ships he traveled on for twenty-five years, soaked in DDT and chlordane?
The renovations we did in Baltimore, sanding off lead paint
and ripping out asbestos? The stress I caused him by teaching

a semester in Europe, leaving him alone with his new business? Forty percent of cancers are preventable; 60 percent are not. Of the fifty trillion cells in a human body, millions are mutating at any given time, but several mutations must occur before a cell turns into a malignancy. When we think about the causes of cancer, environment and heredity represent two points on a triangle. Randomness is the third point, although of course randomness could merely be a label for forces we don't yet understand. Cancer, Susan Sontag argues, is "a disease or pathology of space. Its principal metaphors refer to topography." We refer to the disease spreading or diffusing, while we deny the fact that cells are always mutating. We enter the space of cancer as if it is isolated from our usual domain.

I remember looking up "peripheral T cell lymphoma" and feeling the information shoot up my body like electricity. And then sink into my gut like a lead basketball. Multiple disease relapses. Aggressive. Fast-growing. Hard to cure. Stem cell transplant. Palliative radiation. Salvage chemo. The last brought up images of a warehouse filled with junk from crashed buses and derailed trains. And then immediately, even as I was reading, I imagined life without Tyrone. I imagined dating a woman I knew. Tyrone would live three more years, and I was already imagining him dead.

Oscar Wilde said, "There is a luxury in self-reproach. When we blame ourselves, we feel no one else has a right to blame us." I have asked myself whether I am confessing to be absolved. But no, I am not reproaching myself as much as exposing myself. I am writing, as Jung said, to make the unconscious conscious. To not believe in fate.

When Tyrone was in hospice care at home, he asked me to invite friends for a party. "I want to see them while I am alive," he said. "I won't be at the funeral." We ate and drank and our guests said goodbye, tears in their eyes.

A few days later I heard him on the phone with my best friend who lives two thousand miles away. "So, when are you coming to visit me?"

She arrived, and the next night Tyrone was so restless I put more fentanyl patches on his back so we could both sleep. I didn't realize that his restlessness was a sign of imminent death. And I didn't know that the extra dose of opiate would prevent him from being able to speak. His last chance to do so. What would he have said?

Tyrone's last gift to me was to die while my friend was with us. And to wait until I had climbed into our bed to hold his hand.

I miss Tyrone, every day. Sometimes I want to tell him something: *You were right about the tiles.* Or I want to ask him what he remembers about a certain dinner. I yearn for him to taste the Asian pears from the tree we planted.

Frazer's *Golden Bough* describes two kinds of magic. Metaphoric magic requires an effigy of the person, like a photograph. Metonymic magic requires taking a piece of the person. Metonyms are substitutions, and by considering what we substitute, we can access our deepest—and often invisible—values. We name and rename things because we don't already possess them.

Sometimes I find Tyrone's handwriting on a canceled check or a note. This substitute for his being causes me to gasp a little, not just because *the hand* is important, distinctly his. "Write" comes from Old English, as does "writhe," to twist, as in agony. One added letter: a breath's difference. The small and specific evidence of his hand propelled by a beating heart causes me more grief than any photograph. Perhaps because that scrap of paper is a piece of ephemera I might, without a pang of guilt, throw away.

Line upon Line

because we knew / It was the spirit that we sought

—WALLACE STEVENS, "THE IDEA OF ORDER AT KEY WEST"

I GREW UP A HEATHEN, A WORD WHOSE ETYMOLOGY means "inhabiting open country." Although my parents and I always lived in or near cities, the image of uncultivated land without fences or other human structures is a fair representation of my lack of religious education. Baptized Catholic in Munich, Germany, I was never confirmed, and the only instruction I recall occurred when neighbors invited five-year-old-me to Sunday school with their daughter. That morning, we constructed trivets from popsicle sticks on which we pasted coloring-book images of a blue-eyed Jesus. My parents looked askance at the trivet I brought home, and I never went to Sunday school again.

As the youngest of six children, growing up Catholic in Slovenia, my father had the choice—as in Stendhal's *The Red and the Black*—of becoming a priest or attending the military academy in Belgrade. He chose the latter. He liked to tell this story: When the Catholic church in South Bend, Indiana, required him to tithe, he asked if the church would care for my mother and me if he died. The "no" was the end of St. Matthew's for him.

At ten, a friend asked me my religion. I ventured, "My father is Catholic and my mother is Protestant."

"That must be hard," my friend replied. "What denomination?"

I didn't know. At home, I asked my mother, and she laughed, "Catholic, of course." But why did she not attend church? We ate lamb (which I hated) at Easter and we had a Christmas tree, but I didn't read the Bible until college. We didn't even own one, except my father's, in Slovenian.

Until I moved to Utah, religion didn't affect me. It was an institution to which other people, including my best friend, subscribed, with me watching curiously from a distance. After twenty years as a corporate attorney, that friend earned a divinity degree and then found more meaningful work as an Episcopal priest. I liked reading her sermons, which began with scripture, illustrated via contemporary or personal anecdote, and ended with reflections on generosity, kindness, love—and faith.

The word "science" comes from Latin, *scire*, "to know." Science is based on evidence. The word "religion" comes from Latin, *religare*, "to bind." The institution of religion makes people behave, and while it should also facilitate a relationship with God, there's no guarantee that it will.

As an adult I asked people why they believed what they did, or how they chose a group to worship with. Another friend wanted to become an Episcopal priest, but his German parish did not recommend homosexuals for the priesthood, so he channeled energy into becoming a Jungian analyst while remaining devout. Interestingly, neither of my younger cousins, raised to be good Catholics, is a believer, and their mother, my ninety-two-year-old aunt, recently told me she is agnostic and no longer goes to church. She cited abuse by priests as the reason, but there might have been no reason for her religiosity—except habit and desire for community—in the first place.

I gathered information about everything, including religion and ethics, by reading. I read and reread *Paradise Lost* and *The Tibetan Book of the Dead*. In the Buddhist text, I scanned the steps, deities, furies, and directions, but I held onto the idea that we are living and dying every day, and that lines between life and death are permeable. The book's concluding paean to virtue and goodness could be an Episcopal sermon.

Paradise Lost ("Go, for thy stay, not free, absents thee more") changed my syntax, a bodily shift from the subject-verb-object strictures of contemporary English. Grammar is conventional not unlike the way that gender is conventional, a set of learned behaviors. When we follow the rules, we are rewarded by recognition and belonging. *Paradise Lost* complicated my thinking. Reading it in my thirties was the first time I understood that the rhythms of language convey meaning ancillary to or sometimes even separate from the content of the words. "Can it be a sin to know?" is the central question of Milton's epic, as it recasts the biblical fall from paradise into part war of the worlds and part domestic drama where Eve is beguiled into sin, after which Adam sins deliberately in order to stay with her. The fact that Milton made Eve more gullible and less culpable than she is in the Bible can be seen as chivalric or sexist, or both.

These days, some parents attempt to raise their children without gender by giving them androgynous names and pronouns and by avoiding gendered toys, clothes, and activities. Gender-free child-rearing is difficult because gender is a public performance. Couples have gender-reveal showers for their fetuses. People expect an answer to "girl or boy?" They less often ask about religion. Our Christmas tree, alongside the absence of other artifacts and behaviors, gave friends and neighbors the impression that we were Christian. Perhaps many families use religious artifacts without a core of belief. In any case, I found my own way in this one aspect of identity.

At eighteen, home from college for Christmas, I paid for a session with a psychic who read palms. Born with myriad fine and deep lines on my palms and foot soles (a genetic condition inherited from my mother), I wondered what a palm reader would say about them. Palmistry was one of the ways I sought to understand who I was or could be: at fifteen I'd bought a computer-generated chart informing me that, in addition to a Gemini sun, I had the moon in Cancer, Sagittarius rising, Venus in Taurus, and Mercury in Gemini. I consulted these certainties when I felt confused, which was often. Sagittarius rising meant, for example, that I experience life as a quest for meaning, and that I need an outlet for my energies. The generality of the wisdom nuggets didn't discourage me. On a mission to understand myself and others, I was as fervid as a badger digging for a vole and as stealthy, for my parents (I thought) didn't have a clue about the hobbies to which I devoted so many hours.

I also started analyzing handwriting. With graphology books spread out in front of me, I would create a portrait of the person from their script, looking at spacing, shape, slant, and letter formation. A blank page allows the hand, ambassador for the body, to express feelings: about the past, the future, about giving and taking, about saying "I." I even consciously altered my own handwriting to align with how I wanted to be: eliminating the affected cap on the lowercase *a* and using a single-stroke capital *I*. I didn't know then that graphology is a pseudoscience, a way of knowing that cannot be proven.

The forty-minute appointment with the psychic palm reader, a suburban housewife, took place in the airy kitchen of her colonial in Bergen County, New Jersey. She had come recommended by a friend with whom I shared not only a quest for self-knowledge but a sense of unfulfillment. We yearned for a *Mademoiselle* whirl of parties with boys professing endless love at the same time that we nurtured arcane passions and refused to smooth the edges of our intellects in order to attract boys.

I was a slate on which crisscrossed two very different kinds of writing, the 1970s dominant culture's block type and the often illegible cursive of my own oddities. I thought I could find out everything I needed to know. While I had (secretly) chosen the University of Virginia in part because the ratio of men to women (eight to one) favored my getting dates with men, after a fraternity party the first week of college, boys in Docksiders and chinos drinking Kool-Aid laced with grain alcohol dropped off my list of interests. At the same time, in a first-year seminar called "Sense and Nonsense in the Game of Reading," the brilliant and wacky professor sat cross-legged like a Buddha on the coffee table in the dorm's basement lounge, reciting Wallace Stevens's poem "The Idea of Order at Key West" or William Blake's "The Garden of Love." Blake's poem describes a locked chapel built on the green, and ends, "Priests in black gowns, were walking their rounds / And binding with briars, my joys & desires." It was a poem I, too, memorized. Blake's unconventional (for his era) ideas included sexual and racial equality, and his mysticism encouraged me to delve more deeply into realms beyond here and now. Perhaps many teenagers are obsessed with divination at this time in their lives when anything seems possible yet little can be attained. The word "divination" has as its root *divus*, godlike, because gods know what humans don't.

In Greek mythology, three fates are responsible for determining someone's thread of life: Clotho spins it, Lachesis draws it out, and Atropos cuts it. In the Bible, Job 14:5–6 reads, "A person's days are determined; you have decreed the number of his months and have set limits he cannot exceed. So look away from him and let him alone, till he has put in his time like a hired laborer." This suggests that God determines a person's life span but not her fate. The psychic was careful to preface her remarks with something like, "Nothing I tell you cannot be altered by your own actions." I remember little else of what she said, except for one thing, "You will find your soul mate in middle age." I must have looked horrified about the wait, because she quickly added, "Don't worry, you will love and be loved, it's just that this relationship will be different." Given the divorce rate in the United States, her prediction could have just been a good bet.

The word "soul" refers to a spiritual essence distinct from the body; its etymology comes from the word for sea, reflecting the ways Germanic and pre-Celtic peoples believed that souls emerge and return to sacred lakes, a belief that also speaks to the primacy of water as a source and sustainer of life. In Greek, *pneuma* is breath or life, while *psyche* means soul or spirit, evincing that bodies are not the only aspect of human life, that the immaterial and unseen also matter.

Our use of the word "matter" to mean "significant" points to
how much we weigh what can be weighed, perhaps exactly
what led Duncan McDougall in 1901 to weigh bodies before
and after death, concluding that the soul weighs twenty-one
grams. Alas, his experiments have not been validated. Today,
most people do not expect a "soul" to have weight. Indeed,
science has no evidence for the soul; quantum physics, for
example, would demand proof in the form of an observable
particle.

The notion of the soul has been promulgated by former
Catholic monk and Jungian therapist Thomas Moore, whose
book *Care of the Soul* was followed, in 1993, by *Soul Mates:
Honoring the Mysteries of Love and Relationship*, which argues that when we use the term to refer to friends or spouses,
we are honoring deep, ineffable relationships. "All intimate
relationships require magic, because magic, not reason and
will, accomplish what the soul needs," writes Moore. Maybe
the word "magic" stands in for "love," and thus Moore's insight is commonplace. Or, because one difficult-to-define
term (magic) relates to another one equally difficult (soul),
the sentence is like a Buddhist koan, impossible to parse.
Granted, writing about spirituality is frustrating because
there is much we don't have words for. Moore's omission
of same-sex unions dates his book, as do his entirely white
and middle-class examples, which he justifies on the basis of
his own standpoint. He seems to believe that deep relationships—like the soul that facilitates them—can exist outside
of culture. His definition of "soul" implies transcendence
of earthly, quotidian complications such as race and gender. He doesn't address the contradiction implied in giving
something ethereal "a mate." Isn't the very notion of "mating"

rooted in our bodies? Moore lists both friends and spouses as soul mates, but he doesn't discuss the confluence of gender and desire when two people of the same sex are married to each other. Does being the same sex double the soul mate potential? Or is the yin/yang of complementarity more desirable? Or is gender not supposed to matter in a soulful relationship? Reading the book a quarter of a century after its publication, I'm struck by its determined otherworldliness, as if a generic place of unmarked identity—from which we can operate and achieve our potential—exists.

Five years after seeing the psychic, I fell in love with Tyrone, a Jamaican British immigrant. I didn't wonder whether Tyrone was my soul mate, but I was so in love with him I was willing to defy my parents—and our culture—to live with him. We married after years of living together, a Baltimore City Hall formality so that I could be included on his health insurance and that I could say "my husband" without blushing. He jokingly called me "trouble and strife," Cockney rhyming slang for "wife." In Washington, DC, common-law marriage can be recognized after as little as six months of cohabitation, a law that helps women hold fathers accountable for their children, but Maryland didn't recognize our union, and certainly not for health insurance. Marriage, like religion, is an institution I am suspicious of; like the Transcendentalists, I believe that institutions corrupt human beings.

After Tyrone and I had been together nearly twenty years, in order for me to take a teaching position at Westminster College in Salt Lake City, he quit his job as a country club chef and we moved from Baltimore to the largest American desert, the Great Basin, 206,162 square miles bounded by the Sierra

Nevada on the west, the Wasatch Mountains on the east, the Sonoran highlands to the south, and the Columbian Plateau to the north. Neither of us had ever lived in a desert, and the high mountains and their proximity stunned us with their grandeur, while the dry climate proved a welcome change. We bought a 1965 tract house in the foothills, and it would be years before we understood the peculiar terrain of our plot of land, the thin layer of arid and alkaline topsoil covering debris from construction, and bedrock. We gradually gave up on plants that had done well in Baltimore, such as azaleas, hydrangeas, and heathers. The rivers and streams of the Great Basin flow into salt lakes, where the water stagnates, evaporates, or sinks into the earth, making the soil alkaline. Because the area was once covered by ocean, archaeologists can find four-hundred-million-year-old coral rugosa. Arches National Park, with its picturesque red rock formations, sits on a bed of salt up to fifteen thousand feet thick.

In this desert valley, however, everything is green in the summer, every tree, every lawn irrigated and fertilized. When I asked the director of Salt Lake water services why water isn't more expensive to discourage people from wasting it, she shrugged. "It doesn't cost us much. The mountains are close." The disjunction between desert and emerald-green lawns makes me angry. It seems like a sin to waste water in a desert, but no law forbids profligate use of water, as long as we pay for it.

There are, of course, plenty of laws in Utah, many of them religiously based, although not enough laws that protect the environment. People from elsewhere are surprised to learn that Salt Lake City is ranked seventh worst in the nation for air pollution, sixth for short-term particulate pollution. This creates a brown blanket over the valley, a cold, baby shit–colored mist in winter. Windshield wipers smear it. That's what we breathe, thanks to pro-business state policies that permit industries to pollute and don't make public transportation a priority. Coal burning is the primary source of electrical power in Utah, and particulate matter is made of soot, from diesel and coal burning, dust, and vehicle emissions. The smallest particles, PM2.5 (one-thirtieth the size of a human hair), are most concerning because they can be inhaled deeply, obstruct the absorption of oxygen, and then aggravate heart and lung diseases. Children are most susceptible, although a friend tells me about a nonsmoking patient with black lung—from living in Salt Lake City.

My anger about the disparity between our gorgeous landscape and the way it is treated might more properly be directed at something else in this culture I live in: the bad behavior resulting from a disjunction between myth and reality, or religion and science. When I marched and distributed literature for abortion rights in Baltimore in the 1980s and 1990s, I encountered people whose religion caused them to oppose me. I thought they were benighted. Didn't they know that the Catholic Church's anti-abortion stance dated only to the beginning of the twentieth century? That in the nineteenth century, ministers and the American Medical Association claimed power over women's bodies? That this power then became law? Still, those decades when I was advocating for abortion rights, I could mostly ignore religion as an institution. Then we moved to Utah, essentially a theocracy because 60 percent of the people in the state, including most of the legislators, belong to one fundamental religion, the Church of Jesus Christ of Latter-Day Saints, also known as the Mormon Church. Of course there are countries that have always been theocracies, but I assumed the United States was safe from religious control of government. Now, after twenty years in Utah, and considering the evangelicalism of Deep South state legislatures and our vice president, I think I was naïve. The reign of religious control in Utah might well forecast the future of the United States.

Over fourteen years, from 1830 to 1844, Joseph Smith created a new American religion, a marvelous—and by that adjective I convey admiration for both his chutzpah and his visionary detail—Protestant hybrid of evangelism and capitalism. When I first moved to Utah I fixated on the sensational aspects of Smith's life and on the fact that the golden tablets on which the Book of Mormon was originally written have never been found. "Oh yeah," I'd say, "how does something like that just disappear?" But during the years I've lived here, I've come to understand all religion as myth, and I no longer single out Mormonism for its mythmaking. Feeding five thousand people with five loaves of bread and two fish? Recorded in all four Gospels—does that mean it is a good story or a factual one?

Tyrone was not religious either. He quoted Marx: "Religion is the sigh of the oppressed creature, the heart of a heartless world, and the soul of soulless conditions. It is the opium of the people." The heart of a heartless world: religion can be one human attempt to make us behave better toward one another; education can be another. Religion melds the unexplainable (a virgin birth, disappeared golden tablets, love) with law. Tyrone's mother practiced Obeah for healing, alongside Christianity. When he got lymphoma, she said he had been cursed. For what or by whom I do not know, but

I suspect his lack of faith was a factor in her mind. Neither Tyrone nor I turned to religion when he became ill, although we tried herbal medicine, visualization, and positive thinking, along with conventional therapies. During those three years, my sense that he would die sometimes felt like a stone I was trying to push out of my head; other times, like water, an intuition seeping into me.

For months after he died, I dreamt of Tyrone speaking to me, even touching me, the physicality of his presence waking me from sleep. This is not uncommon, I know, as one grieves. In response to a death, many people say, "It was his time." Perhaps this notion comforts, because it relieves individuals of responsibility, blame, worry. Or is it just something we say without understanding the implication? Muslims say, "Inshallah," if God wills it, like the Episcopalians' "God willing." Thinking God is in charge comforts us, because even if terrible things happen, they happen for a purpose or beyond our control. "Thank God" might also be what J. L. Austin terms a speech act, words that enact what they say, warding off the evil eye just in case there happens to be a God watching.

Three months after Tyrone died, I had dinner with Laura. I'd met her eight years earlier at one of the poetry readings I organize. "Who are you?" I'd said, as she was trying to exit the auditorium and I was gathering people for the reception. She was striking: tall and strong, with thick hair the color of autumn stalks of corn, and blue eyes. "I'm nobody," she replied, echoing Emily Dickinson. In her twenties she had earned an MFA from Mills College, and she wanted to continue her involvement with the literary world far from her job as a

technical writer. She became a regular in the poetry community, volunteering with a summer conference that I helped
organize. I invited her to join the conference board during
a hike in the hills above Salt Lake. The rhythm of walking
facilitates speech, negotiating a path creates intimacy, and an
outdoor landscape makes the walk public but also private. I
knew Laura was lesbian, and I found her beautiful, but I kept
the attraction to myself.

Until, after Tyrone's death, I invited her for a dinner of
homemade pizza. During that long evening, I learned about
trauma in her past. I mostly listened, in part because I had a
respiratory infection and coughed a lot. That was not at all
romantic, and although I remember feeling very tired, I also
wanted her to stay, like watching a film with a riveting plot. I
was listening to her with every pore in my body open. In an
email later she apologized for staying so long, and I replied,
"If I had wanted you to leave, I would have let you know. I'm
nothing if not direct." The evening reset our relationship. I
already knew that her spiritual practice—which she calls "a
path"—asked her to be vegetarian. That evening I realized
that every other thing about her also expressed tenderness,
the kind that melts the heart of anyone needing it, which of
course is everyone. From working with her I knew that she
was trustworthy, but that night I learned that she was also
too trusting, as when her loyalty clouds any sense of others'
motives and flaws. I had been attracted to many women in
the past, and I'd even made passes at some, but I had never
before chosen a woman who was interested in me at the very
moment I was interested in her.

"Interlace your fingers in the nonhabitual way," the yoga
teacher says, and it takes a few seconds to figure out what

that is. The right pinkie newly nestled between the left one and the ring finger of the left hand, the left thumb under the right. Same fingers, same hands, but the nonhabitual way feels new. *Yoga* is the Sanskrit word for "yoke," the union of mind and body, and it presumes that the body can retrain the brain. Or vice versa. Our first kiss that spring made me feel like a teenager in an aging body. But whether it was because Laura was a woman or because she wasn't Tyrone, I don't know. I had been a faithful wife. I spoke of my attractions only to my closest friends, telling them about a crush on my aerobics teacher or the way I would scan a room and count the people I was attracted to: two men, one woman, or vice versa, or someone in between, keeping the pulse of my pansexuality at the same time that I stored it away. Yet my second book of poems is titled *Bend,* and one of the poems contains the lines, "bend / and make the horizon disappear / ...feet are not straight / belly is not." Adrienne Rich proposed that women exist on a lesbian continuum, that it's not genital activity but a woman's resistance to compulsory heterosexuality that counts.

"How did you move from friend to lover?" someone asked me, about Laura. It was like slipping into a pool of water that I thought would be cool but was warm. It was like interlacing my fingers in the nonhabitual way. I later called up my lesbian friends and asked, "Why didn't you tell me?" Why didn't they tell me the sex would be great and the relationship easy? Whether it felt easy because we were already friends or because she was female, or because I had only my marriage to Tyrone for comparison, or because we were both past our moody youths, I don't know. In any case, my timing was lucky: a later-in-life love with a woman who didn't seek a youthful body and for whom I seemed wise, more traveled, more tempered, the way steel is tempered, over time and with heat, into a new shape. At the point in my life where, because of aging, I was feeling invisible, I found love again. In the gay male community, the "Dorian Gray syndrome" is arguably worse; in the lesbian community, arguably better, because women are valued for their experience and character.

After I started dating Laura, I hosted a Mother's Day brunch for mothers and daughters. Someone brought foil-wrapped chocolates, and Laura, who sat next to my mother, turned the wrappers into bright origami cranes. My mother picked one up and admired it—she too made beautiful things: curtains, pillows, precisely tailored clothes, dolls. Laura charmed my mother by paying very close attention to her, and I suspect my mother sensed that this new woman in my life would try to please her as well as me.

When the guests were leaving, I offered them parsley plants from my yard. Two flat-leaf parsley plants I'd bought for the thin, rocky soil of my garden had multiplied into thousands. The Latin name for parsley, *petroselinum*, comes from the Greek word for stone, *petro*, because parsley could grow on stony hills in Greece. In the summer months, passersby probably think the parsley plants are weeds, as they look dried out, yellow, and gone to seed. They mix with the lupines that also turn crisp and yellow in the hot months, while they are seeding themselves. New parsley plants come up in spring and fall, while in the summer I can only harvest the crop by trimming plants of their mature and tough side leaflets. Unlike rosemary or basil, parsley doesn't do well in pots—it needs the terroir of the soil—and so, after the first hard frost, it is either buried under the snow or visible but frozen, its cells broken into glassy chlorophyll wetness, good only for flavoring soup.

Parsley plants spring up where I least expect them, in the most unwelcoming crevice, for instance between stepping-stones. One area some five feet in diameter under a pine tree where nothing has grown before is thick with hip-high parsley plants. I offered these plants to my guests, but I knew that if their soil was better than mine, the herb would not taste as good. Although Horace wrote, "Skies change, souls don't," suggesting that character dominates milieu, he also wrote, "Adversity has the effect of eliciting talents, which in prosperous circumstances would have lain dormant." This is true for parsley, whose apiol essence is intensified through the adversity of poor soil. Perhaps it was also true for me.

My mother joined me in digging. Kneeling on the ground, she asked, "Are you with that woman?"

"Yes," I said.

"Well, she's very nice. And smart too, I think," my mother said. How did my mother know? Had she noticed the way Laura attended to her—paying close attention is a kind of intelligence—or perceived Laura's deft analysis of Vermont's legalization of same-sex marriage after the governor's veto? Laura, who had never been married, saw marriage equality as a step forward for human rights. Perhaps my mother was just relieved to see me happy again, or perhaps she'd learned something from my father's rejection of Tyrone, but she moved into my new relationship as easily as I had. I felt I had been given a limitless extension on the paper I was writing about love, although in 2009, I did not imagine that in a few years *Oberfell v. Hodges* would make same-sex marriage legal everywhere in the United States, even in Utah.

In contraband videos posted on YouTube of meetings of the twelve apostles of the LDS church, I watched old white men sit in comfortable chairs and discuss issues of 2008. In one clip, titled "on religious freedom," the apostles discuss their support of California's Proposition 8, against same-sex marriage. The former governor of Utah testifies in support. Political analyst Fred Karger followed the infusion of money and manpower needed to pass Prop 8, discovering that the LDS faithful had contributed $30 million. Some even traveled to California to canvass door-to-door in favor of the law. All this despite the fact that in the United States, a church's non-profit status forbids it to "intervene in political campaigns" or to "attempt...to influence legislation."

The *LDS Doctrine and Covenants* state that the world is seven thousand years old, but I have come to understand that not all Mormons—maybe even not most—are in lock-step with doctrine. Not every member of the LDS church agreed with Prop 8, and not every member of the church is a literalist. At a symposium at Brigham Young University, one speaker offered the image of time from John McPhee's *Basin and Range:* "With your arms spread wide again to represent all time on earth, look at one hand with its line of life...in a single stroke with a medium-grained nail file you could eradicate human history." Shivering at this image of human insignificance, I acknowledge the complexity of generalizing about what Mormons—what anyone—believe. Years and millennia are as artificial as everything else humans construct. The grammar of English, anchored in past, present, and future tenses, does not facilitate understanding the complicated, layered, and individualized way that time is perceived. According to physicist Carlo Rovelli, time is different depending on where we are and how fast we are moving, and also *who* we are: time is a function of individual memory. Each individual consciously negotiates between self and other, known and unknown, fact and myth, creating a system of beliefs, but they also—less consciously—create their experience of time.

Joseph Smith was jailed and then later murdered by a mob in Nauvoo, Illinois, for destroying a rival's printing press about to disclose his polygamy. Mormon pioneers arrived without Smith in the Mexican territory of Utah. On July 24, 1847, Brigham Young, sick with Rocky Mountain spotted fever, looked out from a wagon that passed through what is now Emigration Canyon in Salt Lake City, and said, "It is enough. This is the right place." That is myth—there's no evidence of Young's statement. However, a theme park now marks "the place" and July 24 is Pioneer Day, a state holiday featuring a parade and fireworks more elaborate than those on July 4. Non-Mormons call it "Pie and Beer Day." The quip reveals the sharp divide between believers and gentiles (anyone who is not Mormon) in Utah.

You might think a religion eager to proselytize would want their members to mix with nonmembers. But during the time I've lived here, I've been invited to exactly two Mormon households, despite the fact that at first I invited many Mormons to my house. Is my resentment a throwback to middle-school cliquishness? As I'm wondering, I realize that Mormon obligations to family and church are like a full-time job, leaving little free time. On Sundays alone, they spend at least two hours (recently changed from four) at the ward church, listening to official interpretations of scripture, without debate or questioning. An LDS student from Vermont

told me that, in her opinion, large Utah congregations produce "thoughtlessly following" adherents. These congregations also inculcate uniformity and facilitate surveillance.

I'm a city person, I say, when I reflect on the places I've
lived, because I gain energy from the differences between
my neighbors and me, because I like the surprising juxta-
positions that cities encourage, say, a tiny salon for eyebrow
threading next to a Jamaican patty take-out joint. In the center of Salt Lake City, across the street from the LDS Temple,
there is a new shopping mall with over a hundred national
retailers and restaurant chains. Its Sunday closure is one sign
of its LDS financing; another, I would argue, is the lack of
local merchants. The LDS church determined the tenants of
the mall it paid for. Such control is linked to a 1970s policy
of "correlation" in which the church decides everything from
the architecture of buildings to how theology will be taught.
This micromanaging policy exists comfortably in the gap
produced by the state of Utah's lack of business regulation.

The LDS compound in Salt Lake includes a part of Main
Street that was bought by the church from the city as an ease-
ment in 2003. Walking through this portion of Main Street
with his skateboard under his arm, one of my students was
escorted out by security guards grasping his elbows. In 2009,
when Matthew Aune and Derek Jones kissed while walking
through, they were arrested for trespassing, although the city
later dropped the case because the church had not posted
clear "private property" signs. Signs are posted now, so if
Laura and I walked through and stopped to kiss, we could
be arrested and fined up to a thousand dollars. Actually, we
avoid places where we might clash with whoever is in charge,

including the grounds of Temple Square. I wonder if any of the twelve apostles of the LDS church ever avoids entering a space—not because they don't want to enter it, but because they are afraid.

Interestingly, because Salt Lake City is the largest city for five hundred miles in every direction, it attracts gay people: ex-Mormons who don't want to leave home as well as newcomers who love outdoor recreation or need jobs. For some, it is possible to thrive within the liberal footprint of Salt Lake County and ignore, accept, or combat the theocracy that runs the state. I asked a queer activist professor who has been at the University of Utah for thirty years how she likes Utah. "I love it. I can make a difference here," she said. "I might be the only openly gay person my Mormon students meet." I wonder why I don't feel I can make a difference in Utah, where I've lived longer than anywhere else in my life. There is a freedom in being beyond the pale, in not counting because one is not Mormon, while still having a supportive circle of like-minded friends. But it's odd to feel free and stifled at the same time. Perhaps what I am externalizing or projecting onto the Mormon faith—the part of myself I cannot bear—is the part that wants to be right, my ego, also the part of me that thrives in a place of doubt.

I'd like to say that I agree with twentieth-century theologian Paul Tillich that God is not "out there" and separate from me but immanent, *within* me, "the ground of my being." I like to think the world is too beautiful to not also be divine. I want to believe in God as a mystical power whose influence I can't fathom but am prevented by the sense that such belief would be an abdication for me. I appreciate the notion that love is divine, even our reason for being, but I think Christ is a myth. So one term for me is agnostic: I don't know that God exists. I do not have a faith. When asked if he believed in God, Carl Jung famously said, "not believe, *know*," referring to his faith. He later regretted his words because, he said, his quick answer made it seem that belief was simple. "Spiritual but not religious" has become a cliché, with "spiritual" representing a vast array of beliefs about divinity and "higher powers." I am neither spiritual nor religious, but I am driven to know, in whatever ways exist: science, of course, but also mysticism and intuition.

Bedrock is the solid foundation of land, sediment turned into stone, and Mormonism is Utah's metaphorical bedrock. Understanding its nature is vital to living with it, the way vintners in the Rhône valley recognize the mineral content of the soil to grow good grapes. Maintaining lawns in a desert imposes destructive human ego on the earth, much like laws that permit pollution. This may seem obvious, but why, then, do so many people in Utah ignore it? The LDS church has only recently issued a mild statement about climate change: "The state of the human soul and the environment are interconnected, with each affecting and influencing the other." The issue might be that the church cares more about an eternal afterlife than here and now. Both heaven and earth are patriarchal. Although as a territory, and then as a state, Utah gave women the right to vote back in the nineteenth century, most historians see this as a ploy to increase the Mormon vote. LDS females are trained to be submissive to men and the entirely male church hierarchy. One in five Utah women uses antidepressants, almost twice the national average. One in three Utah women will experience domestic violence, compared to one in four nationwide. Mormons are encouraged to have as many children as possible. Utah's population growth of 29.6 percent more than doubles that of the nation (13.2 percent), yet Utah ranks fifty-first (including Puerto Rico) in spending on education.

Re = again, *velum* = veil. To remove the veil. To believe in revelation is to believe in truth behind a veil. Mormons believe they pass through a veil at death into the afterlife. They believe that God can speak directly to human beings. Revelation suggests a magician removing a cloth and, *voilà!* The thing one has been waiting for. Conversely, philosopher Jacques Derrida defines truth as a series of shifting veils, *not the thing behind the veil, but the veil itself.* The process, not the product, impossible to hold because it changes so fast. Ptolemy thought the earth was the center of the universe until Galileo proved him wrong. The earth was assumed to be perfectly round until we had more precise ways of measuring. We make human beings conform to one sex or the other because we ignore or destroy evidence of intersex. Scientific truth—all truth—exists to be questioned. In a theocracy, however, curiosity and questioning are not virtues.

The college where I teach has no religious affiliation, and most of the faculty members are not LDS. Westminster professors agree that we can teach texts that rile conservative students, most of whom are from Utah. But we face repercussions. Almost every semester a few students complain about a book I've chosen. Early in my time at the college, it was Toni Morrison's *Sula.* "Sex is private and sacred," said an older student, "and shouldn't be discussed in a classroom." Three others agreed. Before I took this job, I taught for twenty years at several institutions, including Johns Hopkins, Goucher

College, and the University of Maryland, and never before had students complained about sexual material. The sex scene between Sula and her best friend Nel's husband is not explicit, but Sula takes the initiative, and the novel questions gender roles, women's sexuality, and morality. Sula is an artist without a genre; born forty years later into a different family, she would have been a flower child, a Black Panther, a Toni Morrison. *Sula* questions how culture determines life paths. In *Sula*, the reader feels the possibilities trapped within the main character, the fluidity of human nature against the rigidity of ideology, those lines in stone. How can sex be private if some of the ways one can have sex break laws? My student, of course, was thinking not about homosexual sex, but about what he shared with his wife. On the contrary, I believe that today nothing is private, although historically the concept meant "not counted." Put another way, the Greeks used the word "private" to indicate insignificance. In Utah, women are in danger of insignificance *and* having our secrets accessed.

With the help of gerrymandering, Utah's two senators and five congresspersons are all Mormon. So are the governor, lieutenant governor, Salt Lake County mayor, attorney general, and the entire alcohol control board, along with 85 percent of the Utah state House and Senate representatives. The lesbian mayor of Salt Lake City is not Mormon, and neither is most of her council. But the liberal city sits in a chair that is strapped to the state, unable to prevent further desecration of our environment, for example with an "inland port," a distribution hub for goods trucked in from elsewhere. A similar political separation between liberal city and conservative surroundings was reflected in many other states in the last US presidential election.

LINE UPON LINE   151

Why single out Utah for its regressive politics? When food guru Christopher Kimball asked cookbook writer Nigella Lawson what past era she would like to live in, she answered, "None. I'm a woman." Kimball quickly apologized for forgetting misogyny's grip. What about the Minoans? Can any of us imagine what it would be like to live in a matriarchy? A place where women are not required to use what W. E. B. Du Bois calls a double consciousness, seeing themselves as men see them?

Utah, where every Mormon man is doctrinally a priest and a higher percentage of women than men believe that women should not be ordained into the priesthood, is the state whose laws rank forty-ninth (lowest after Arkansas) in being favorable to women. Although the LDS church no longer permits polygamy, the Mormon celestial kingdom is based on the practice. After the Second Coming, souls will be sorted into degrees of glory. Mormons believe that anyone who has led a good life will enter the telestial kingdom. The next level up is the terrestrial. The highest is the celestial kingdom, where Mormon men will have sex with multiple wives who bear many children, populating "spirit worlds without number." In the kingdom, men will be granted their young bodies and have their own planets. Women can only get in if "sealed" (married in the church) to a man and, then, if in the afterlife he chooses them, although Jesus can marry especially virtuous single women. Tyrone was advised not to tell potential employers that his wife's job brought him to Utah because that signaled his weakness, a trait that would prevent him from being hired.

There is a Chinese saying, *Wo ming zai wo, buzai tian:* my fate lies with me, not with heaven. I don't believe in an afterlife, although I would like a second life on earth, to try to be a better person, and not make the same mistakes. Otherwise, I'll keep revising how I live this one. The Torah emphasizes this life and immediate punishments for certain acts, and Jews are free not to believe in an afterlife. Mormons are instructed to believe that the afterlife is eternal and all-important. As a person who usually delays gratification in favor of future rewards, I should be able to understand that, but I can't. I believe I have only one chance to live, a belief that raises the stakes for *now*.

Many Mormons believe that homosexuality is a choice, that children can be "recruited" into it, and that it can be "cured." Mormons have a name for counseling and/or electroshock to "cure" gay people of their same-sex attraction: "reparative therapy." The LDS church owned a nonprofit counseling company called Evergreen until it closed in 2014. Evergreen, which ran camps to convert queer people, was replaced by a new organization—North Star, which purports to offer "support" for LGBT members and family. One friend told me that the Evergreen camp proved to him that his attraction to men could *not* be changed. Another friend found his partner there. Apostle David Bednar expects Mormons to "not act on" their same-sex attraction, but the church also expects everyone to marry (the opposite sex), creating many unhappy marriages. Every religion's doctrine changes, but Mormonism is sluggish. I imagine the twelve apostles carving a line in rock about women's and gay rights because they are threatened by a world different from their own. I don't know if Utah will be teased out of its theocracy by the influx of newcomers and by declining numbers of the faithful, or if the theocracy will hold steady while the rest of the country reverts to more stringent antiwoman laws, with the patriarchy safely back in charge.

The *Odyssey* contains many predictions, most famously that Odysseus will return home to Penelope. Evil characters disregard prophecies, wise ones like Telemachus trust them, but no characters control their own lives and determine their fates. Omens and prophecies are the gods' way of showing humans their powerlessness. Anything could have meaning in the ancient world: entrails, the sky, birds. When I recently met my first blue heron on a Gulf of Mexico beach, it stood three feet tall, just an arm's length from me walking past three men with a cooler full of beer. "I chased it away but it came back," one of the men said when I asked what kind of bird it was.

"Why did you chase it away?"

The man pointedly didn't answer my question. Maybe the heron was hoping the group would start fishing, having learned that groups of men do this. Maybe the man chased the bird away because he was unnerved by being so closely watched.

The next day, the men were gone but the heron stood in the same place on the beach, looking at me as I passed. For the Chinese, the heron is a symbol of strength, patience, and long life. Indeed, herons can live fifteen years. Ancient Egyptians thought they meant prosperity. Some African tribes think they communicate with the gods. Surely this heron meant something—why would it have been in the same place two days in a row, nodding its graceful head at me, at a time when I was struggling to finish a difficult project? In the moment I read it as a sign intended for me, I ignored its own territorial nature.

Astrology, tarot, palm reading, Ouija, numerology—the many kinds of divination underscore our yearning to know. When I was younger, I sought occult ways of knowing, although I didn't take what I learned to be true "for time and all eternity," the Mormon phrase used in the marriage ceremony. Rather, my discoveries existed as pieces seen in turns of a kaleidoscope; they changed as I did. As a teenager, Joseph Smith used seer stones to translate the Book of Mormon. Attempting to see what is hidden—predicting the future through astrology, for instance—presumes a power that belongs to God and is thus condemned by both mainstream Protestants and Catholics. Yet seeing what is hidden—finding evidence—is also one function of science.

Some fraudulent psychics use internet sleuthing to fool their audiences, and most psychics make claims that could apply to anyone, for instance by foreseeing trauma. The fact that humans find something relevant to themselves in whatever they read or are told is called the Forer Effect, after the scientist who proved it. I wonder, however, if psychics access the intuition all humans are born with but gradually learn to disregard. Do psychics just pay very close attention, akin to the way that gay people learn to recognize one another? Everything about us reveals us, especially our bodies. I believe that every human has the ability to see through someone else's eyes (reading is a version of that) and that people can tap into what another person already unconsciously knows. This might happen when you know someone for a long time—you access their feelings through their body language and other expressions. Some people are more intuitive than others. I'm thinking of a friend who had such a troubled mother that my friend protectively learned to read people's feelings acutely and precisely, like a mind reader. The survival skill she adopted as a child endures as a life skill—not without its burdens, because sometimes it is easier not to know what someone is thinking.

Self-fulfilling prophecy is often used in the negative sense, when someone prevents herself from achieving something she wants, but it is also akin to positive or magical thinking. Magical thinking, argues Matthew Hutson, is something we all do to understand and cope. A related version, circulated by Norman Vincent Peale in the 1950s and then revamped by Rhonda Byrne as *The Secret* in 2006, markets the idea that positive thinking will make it so, that faith in God or the universe can guide us to what we want.

Each culture and era has its diviners: Egyptian court seers, the Oracle of Delphi, the shaman in Asia who reads bones. Reading tarot or the *I Ching* is not antithetical to believing in God or being a Christian, an Episcopalian-Jungian therapist friend tells me. He picks tarot cards to be open to resonances, believing that shuffling the deck creates energetics that we can't rationally explain. I find an online version of the *I Ching*, a ninth-century BCE Chinese book of cleromancy that uses random numbers as a method of divination. Carl Jung believed the *I Ching* and tarot to be useful paths to self- and world-knowledge, a way to access the Collective Unconscious. I virtually threw the coins and got "The Well," number 48: "When we feel a lonely separateness from others, it is not because this Well within has dried up, but because we have lost the means to reach its waters. You need to reclaim the tools necessary to penetrate to the depths of your fellows." Yes, I think, that is what I am trying to do in writing—mend my lonely separateness from others, reclaim

the tools to penetrate their depths! And yet...the next day
I virtually threw the coins again and got "Compulsion," a
warning that I was ignoring a danger to my well-being from
a seduction, a diversion. Was the diversion my attraction to
divination, and a waste of time?

When Laura and I started living together, she told me that
her office was having plumbing work done. The plumber was
the young man who'd bought Tyrone's gray van with its elegant logo of a silver catering dish and lid. Each day for several
weeks, Laura saw the van parked outside her office window.
"He's making sure you're okay," she said, "that I'll love you
well." It comforted her to see the van, and it surprised me. I
hadn't seen the van since the day I sold it. The Salt Lake valley
contains over a million people—what are the chances that
Tyrone's van would be parked outside Laura's office?

Laura, who was raised Catholic and until her twenties
abided by its strictures, for the last twenty-five years has practiced a form of meditation and spiritual practice based on the
teachings of the Sikh Kirpal Singh. Her practice, guided by a
guru, requires seeking a connection to God through light and
sound. She believes in reincarnation, in the spirit world, in an
afterlife. Sometimes I (internally) roll my eyes at these beliefs
at the same time that I remind myself to honor people whose
faith in God is clearer than my own muddy sense that some
power might not be indifferent to humans on earth. Indeed,
Laura's ability to meditate, to believe, to humble her ego, is
part of her appeal for me.

Laura's and my first trip together was to Seattle, a city
neither of us had visited in many years. At the waterfront
Olympic Sculpture Park, we wandered between Claes Olden-

burg's giant eraser and Alexander Calder's red steel eagle. On our way back to the hotel, we discovered a curious rectangular greenhouse. We entered to find an eighty-foot felled western hemlock, trucked there from the Green River watershed as a "nurse log." With help from complex irrigation and air systems, the immense fallen tree supports a new—and ever-changing—cycle of growth: mosses, plants, insects. The metaphor of new life from a dead entity was not lost on us.

Tyrone knew me as no one else will ever know me—because I was younger then, a different person, and also because of who *he* was. My long and complicated relationship with Tyrone made me a better partner for Laura. I resisted marriage with both Tyrone and Laura because it is a phenomenon rooted in the ownership of women. Before same-sex marriage became legal, Laura and I had a lawyer draw up powers of attorney, medical and otherwise, so we did not "need" to be married.

But then I was visiting my priest friend in Richmond when my mother in Utah was admitted to the hospital for a urinary tract infection. Her Alzheimer's made it difficult to reason with or console her, so Laura spent the night in the hospital with her. My friend asked me, "Would Tyrone have spent the night in the hospital with your mother?" The answer was no, even though he was kind to my mother. My friend continued, "So, Laura wants to get married, and why exactly are you holding out?" I swallowed and felt my selfishness move down my gullet like an apricot pit. I married Tyrone for the security of health insurance, and why shouldn't I marry Laura so that she might have similar securities? Surely making a person you love happy is more important than political principle.

When Laura and I started living together, I recalled the psychic's prediction. I wondered if she was my soul mate, if my relationship with her is deeper than my relationship with Tyrone was. I toured a not-yet-dedicated Mormon temple with my mother's Mormon neighbors. I learned that only those married and sealed in the Temple are guaranteed to be reunited after death. I asked the neighbors, "What happens if I remarry? Which mate will be my eternal one?" They smiled and said, "Don't worry. God will decide." On what basis, I wondered. Think of the soul as a space, Thomas Moore says, "an inner space as vast as the outerscape of the universe." This points to possibilities inherent in each of us, but it doesn't explain what happens when one person's vast inner space overlaps with someone else's. I think the psychic used the term "soul mate" in 1973 because she intuited my pansexuality and could not use that word to predict my future. She said that my second significant romantic relationship would be "different" because in 1973, "partner" indicated a law office or business. She used a woo-woo term because she had no other. Or perhaps she told everyone they would meet their soul mate later in life.

After every storm, the Utah sun shines brightly. In late winter the snow hangs heavy from tree limbs that bounce up as the snow melts. The sun evaporates moisture from plowed streets and shoveled sidewalks. The "greatest snow on earth" stays on mountains up to twelve thousand feet high. In June, when the mountains are still snowcapped and the valley below is flowering and green, change seems possible. Surrounded by these mountains, I have learned to always know where (and when) I am. "Live in New York City once, but leave before it makes you hard. Live in Northern California once, but leave before it makes you soft," wrote journalist Mary Schmich. My motto might be, "Live in Utah and do not let it make you, period." Alas, terroir is not just the land but what we do with it. *Terroir* is another word, like *write* and *writhe*, where one letter changes the meaning entirely. I see my own death ahead and realize that I haven't done much to improve the place where I live. I have let the enormity of the enterprise—or other priorities—make me lazy.

Pointing to and looking at the night sky, I know that one fingertip covers millions of galaxies. I may be an alien on this bit of earth surrounded by the built environment and power of the Mormon church. In my longing for open country—a place where religion is not an all-powerful institution—I realize there may not be any. I can also take the long view. The Great Basin will continue to stretch and expand, just like the Atlantic Basin did after North America separated from North Africa. Eventually it will open a breach to the Pacific Ocean, and the Salt Lake will be released to it.

Taste is first and foremost distaste, disgust and
visceral intolerance of the taste of others.

—PIERRE BOURDIEU, *DISTINCTION: A SOCIAL
CRITIQUE OF THE JUDGMENT OF TASTE*

WHEN LAURA FIRST MOVED IN WITH ME, SHE HAD A
group of friends who didn't care about food. More precisely,
they didn't care the way I do. These friends, all gay men
born and raised in Utah, had a lot of parties. Sometimes
the parties were potlucks, and other times they were held at
Stoneground, a restaurant where one of them worked as a
waiter. To please Laura, I ate at Stoneground. I ate pizza with
corn-syrupy-sweet canned marinara and gluey mozzarella
on an underrisen, underbaked crust. I ate wilted salad with
guar-gum-thickened dressing, refrigerated tomatoes, and
flavorless carrots. I ate a dish with vinegary artichokes and
overcooked packaged fettuccine.

"I can't do it anymore," I told Laura. "I can't eat at Stoneground."

"Okay," she said.

Then we were invited to another birthday, also at Stoneground. I offered to bake a carrot cake, the birthday boy's
favorite, as a gift. It is an expensive cake because of the dried
fruit and nuts and the cream-cheese-and-white-chocolate
frosting, but it's easy to make. Through the back door of
Stoneground, I carried the heavy carrot cake on a copper
platter. The twenty-five or so guests oohed and aahed.

Laura ordered eggplant parmesan. When the waiter brought bruschetta for everyone, I was not tempted, in part because I had eaten my usual big lunch and in part because this bruschetta was just canned tomatoes on toasted bread. I enjoyed the conversation and avoided the food.

A few weeks later, Laura let slip that the birthday boy noticed I didn't eat anything except a thin slice of my own cake. "They were offended," she said.

"You know I don't like to eat much at night," I replied. I was reminded of a dinner party we gave where one woman moved food around on her plate and kept exclaiming "delicious," but ate barely a tablespoon of each course. Was I offended? Mostly puzzled, because I knew the food was good. Perhaps she had an eating disorder.

I said to Laura, "I am an adult who must decide what to put into her body." When people try to force other people to eat something they don't like, food becomes the medium for a power play. So many human interactions angle for power and status. What we say or don't say, do or don't do.

"Couldn't you at least have ordered something?"

"I don't like to waste food," I said.

I should have ordered a salad, and if I didn't eat it with relish, "at least picked at it," Laura told me. Maybe there's also something *ur* about refusing food. After all, God preferred Abel's gift of lambs to Cain's gift of garden produce. Because God did not respect Cain and his offering, Cain became so angry he killed his brother.

"You are such a food snob," Laura said.

In grade school the lunch I took to school was a salami sandwich on sourdough rye bread, imported from Canada because no American bakeries made it. This was not sophistication on the part of my parents; it was what they'd grown up with and had learned to prefer. I might have enjoyed white bread with peanut butter, but my starving father had wolfed down a pound of peanut butter after the war, so even the smell later made him sick. My transformation from poor immigrant to food "snob" was the result of the United States embracing the food culture of its immigrants. These days, many cities have bakeries that produce the farmer's loaf of my childhood. Because Salt Lake doesn't have a good bread bakery, I bake my own, using a recipe of Chad Robertson's from the Tartine Bakery in San Francisco, and kamut, spelt, or rye grain I sometimes sprout and then dehydrate and grind myself.

Why snob? Can't we just say enthusiast? Laura likes to tell the story of me elbowing an old man with a cane on my way to sample chocolates in the Valrhona factory store in the Rhône valley. I remember feeling restrained, sly, and excited by all the new varieties waiting for me. A naturopath told me she thinks chocolate works on the deepest level of any food because of the combination of the dark roasted beans and their fat, and the beans' complex blend of neurotransmitters. When chocolate is low in cacao, you don't get these. Phenylethylamine affects blood pressure and pulse, like falling in love. Theobromine (the ingredient that dogs and horses can't metabolize) works like caffeine. Swedish botanist Linnaeus named the cacao tree *theobroma*, food for the gods. Thinking about chocolate's melting point, the soft texture of the cocoa butter, and the fruity dark flavor makes my mouth water. Who first opened a cacao pod and thought to cook the acrid and rubbery seeds, albeit wrapped in a white, sweet membrane? Imagine that person's face tasting those seeds, roasted. I think of Sappho's Fragment 130, "Once again Love, the loosener of limbs, shakes me, that sweet-bitter irresistible creature."

In Baltimore, my friend Albert gave up his chef job, went back to his native Germany, spent six months learning how to make molded chocolates, bought equipment, and then set up shop. My favorites were the earl grey, the whiskey, and the pear Williams. That was more than thirty years ago. I ate so many of Albert's chocolates and learned them so well—like the Scrabble tiles whose wood patterns I memorized for cheating as a child—that I became tired of them. My tastes moved on. Novelty is seductive, and it causes a surge in dopamine. Novelty also represents self-renewal. Whether we buy new clothes or start a love affair, the real change happens in ourselves. The newness can "attain the intensity, if not the quality of the emotion, of love," says critic Jean Baudrillard. We either extend that sublime period or move on to another new thing.

Even Albert's chocolates are too sweet for me now, too familiar, and thus not worth forty dollars a pound. When he started, his competitors were Godiva and Burdick's, and his recipes were cutting-edge. Today, the chocolate world touts bean to bar or tree to bar and fillings flavored with mustard and cardamom and rose petals or fève de tonka, the bean illegal in the United States because it contains the blood thinner (and rat poison and perfume ingredient) coumarin. Tonka beans smell like sweet woodruff and taste like nutmeg, like vanilla, like flowers, and if you ate forty of them you might be sick. Half a bean is enough to flavor chocolate mousse for four.

I discovered fève de tonka in Marseille at Xocoatl Chocolaterie Maino on a short street ironically called the

Grand Rue, where father and son Maino confected three-quarter-inch by half-inch exquisite Valrhona ganache in blends so unusually flavored Laura and I often couldn't guess them. We'd close our eyes and then share a piece, letting the flavors melt over our tongues. A year later we discovered Soma in Toronto. Enveloped in a rarified scent of fair trade, perfectly roasted cacao beans, we chose pralinés from among the flavors of green Iranian raisin, toasted corn, Australian ginger and lemon, Arbequina Spanish olive oil, Douglas fir (shaped like an asymmetrical cone), and eight-year-old balsamic vinegar. Soma doesn't ship. The difficulty of obtaining something adds to its value.

Along with the food section, my favorite parts of the newspaper have always been the columns devoted to ethics, advice, and etiquette. From them—and from the fiction I read—I learned how to be an American, how to be an adult, and how to do the right thing, which, of course, keeps changing. If it is sometimes polite to refuse sweets so as not to appear greedy, other times it is polite to take them and show enjoyment. As a child, refusing food was permissible in what seemed like direct correlation with its desirability. I could say no to chocolate, but not to lamb and green beans. How well I knew the person offering the sweets or the lamb was relevant, as was the time of day, who else was there, and what would happen after the meal. I learned via onsite training but also by reading: *Sue Barton, Nancy Drew, Doctor Dolittle, Little Women*. I was Jo, whose ethical dilemmas pit what she wants against what other people need. Thinking about other people first usually results in being liked.

But how to know what others are thinking? In my thirties, I took the Myers-Briggs personality test and realized that not everyone operated as I did, as an ISTJ. The test, based on the Jungian opposites of introversion/extroversion, sensing/intuition, thinking/feeling, and perceiving/judging, made me realize that all my life I had been hurting people's feelings when I said what I thought or did what I wanted. If I am, as Jung said, becoming my best self as I age, mitigating my introversion and quick judgments, I am still sometimes unsure when to hold my tongue. My contribution to conversations should be *useful*. During one dinner, when I was being interviewed for a job, I told the woman who jogged two hours every morning—while wearing a Walkman—that aerobic activity intensifies acoustic trauma. When I saw a woman at the gym using a machine that my orthopedist thought should be outlawed, I told her what my orthopedist had said. Because the learner in me can never get enough feedback, no matter how negative or inappropriately timed, I make the mistake of thinking that others are like me.

My food snobbery still punctuates my relationship with Laura, although now, years after that Stoneground birthday, our knowledge of each other rarely surprises us. In fact, she now feels free to reject something I've cooked—most recently chocolate chip tahini cookies. I thought they were okay and ate four of them a few minutes out of the oven, but she took one bite, said, "Where's the butter?" and made a face. The cookies did contain butter, but the tahini masked it; it also made their texture puffy and soft instead of chewy and crisp. It seems Laura has become a food snob, too, although I don't know if she would perform her snobbery in front of anyone but me, perhaps because of her family. When we went to lunch at an expensive restaurant with her parents, they whispered to her, "This is not our kind of place." While they earned more money than my parents—Laura's father owned his electrician's business and her mother invested in the stock market—they proudly cling to their working-class origins. Eating at an expensive restaurant is (too) conspicuous consumption, while overbuying and then wasting food at home shows their economic privilege in addition to their lack of planning. My parents, on the other hand, did not think of themselves as working class even when they took jobs as cleaners; moreover, having grown up with good food, it was something they expected to enjoy.

The performance of taste signals the mutable entity of class status, but perhaps the important thing is to ask *why* we perform knowledge in any particular situation. Will it do some good? I've learned a lot about literature and a fair amount about food. In fact, I mostly alternate planning what to eat or cook with thinking about what I'm reading, subjects contiguous only in my head. Roasted nectarine crumble. *I'm two eyes looking out of a suit of armor. I write because I can't talk* (May Swenson). Broad beans with pickled red onion. *We act and walk and speak and talk in ways that consolidate an impression of being a man or being a woman* (Judith Butler). The tissue connecting food and words is my worry about the right thing to make or say, balancing my ideas with other people's feelings.

Erving Goffman's *The Presentation of the Self in Everyday Life* analyzes face-to-face interactions as theater. Through deliberate or unconscious utterances and acts, people reveal aspects of identity to those around them, who might notice, or might not. A situation provides its own rules about what will be ignored or commented on, and how. A guest using the wrong fork at a formal dinner would not be corrected by other guests. Waiters might make fun of customers in the kitchen, but not in the dining room. "Impression management" can mean withholding evidence that might be unfavorably interpreted, or it might mean revealing deceptive evidence—for example, displaying Spinoza's *Ethics* on the coffee table while hiding pornography. Goffman points out that a host pays more attention to how much and how eagerly people eat rather than what they *say* about the food, which suggests that if I had ordered something at Stoneground, I would also have been required to consume it with gusto.

Our ethical positions are complicated by our motives and by the changing nature of truth. Discerning truth means constantly reassessing our stance, just as we reassess our food preferences. Which of our own truths are worth saying or doing? If, while walking, you pass through a swarm of angry bees, you'd tell someone headed that way. But when the danger is not life-threatening—for instance, if you see someone planting a noxious weed—do you speak? I would, but then, that's me. Thus I have a record of getting into trouble by offering what I think are helpful bits of advice. Part of that trouble is created by my class privilege, the one I enjoy now. Or rather, by the way I perform it.

An early poem by Carolyn Forché, "As Children Together," ends, "I have been to Paris / since we parted." I was always bothered by the superiority implied in that last line, perhaps because I replicated it. My ambivalent cosmopolitanism comes from embarrassment about having had opportunities that others may not have had. Travel enlarges what we think is good by increasing the options of consumable items and experiences. So do other kinds of education. One resulting dilemma is deciding when to reveal what we know or like— or, more aptly, what we don't like. Enthusiasm doesn't usually bother anyone; it's negativity that irks.

In his book on improvisation, Keith Johnstone argues that every performance relies on status-raising and -lowering. When someone reveals they know more than someone else, they raise their status. Others respond either by lowering or by raising their own. As a teacher, and especially when teaching issues of race, class, and gender, I keep lowering my status—often by admitting my bafflement and sometimes by offering an example of my own idiocy—so that students feel freer to speak. Figuring out when and how to reveal what you know is a game like the one played by the TV detective Columbo. Gathering information to solve a case, Columbo (Peter Falk) seems naïve or even dumb. People often equated my father's heavy Slovenian accent and occasional grammatical error with a lack of intelligence. Instead of getting defensive, he'd lower his status, saying without irony, "What do I know, I'm a foreigner." And then, when the person he was talking to was disarmed, my father might say, apologetically, "English is the most difficult of the six languages I learned." A power play, of course.

Having the opportunity to choose anything, especially a luxury like expensive chocolate, indicates the privilege of abundance. Choice is a form of power, although too many choices can overwhelm us, as when we stand in front of a wall of vinegars trying to decide between balsamic aged for five or ten or twenty years. Our public choices of what, how, and when to eat help create our class status. I have a friend who turns up her nose at Lindt chocolate (commercial, ubiquitous), and I am sure there are people who reject Valrhona. Although I've seen cacao bushes growing and I've sniffed a raw pod studded with seeds, I haven't studied cacao and chocolate beyond a few minutes of accrued knowledge here and there, along with enthusiastic and increasingly careful consumption. Although I eat chocolate every day, my status as a chocolate connoisseur depends on to whom I'm talking. Compared to the Maino family, I'm a neophyte.

I buy wines by the numbered rating or the price. And although I care about fabrics and the construction and fit of clothes, perhaps because my mother did, I limit myself. Shantung is a wild silk (made with worms that do not have to be killed for harvest) that spots when water touches it. I will not pay seven dollars to have a blouse dry-cleaned each time I wear it. I don't insist on having the best in most things. I'm happy to choose what I like or can afford. In her essay "Against Connoisseurship," novelist Ginger Strand is nostalgic for her grandparents' "tacky" tastes in contrast to her own educated ones. She links travel and wide experiences to the development of taste and the ability to analyze, arguing that "yoking enjoyment to evaluation confuses a striptease with an anatomy lesson."

But wait: can't a striptease *also be* an anatomy lesson? In looking desirously at a body, aren't we learning its contours? Thinking and feeling are closely twined. Why must we turn off learning in order to enjoy something? Strand quotes La Rochefoucauld, "To eat is a necessity, but to eat intelligently is an art." If it's an art, it must be learned. Jung's dichotomies are useful only as a starting point. Connoisseurship means,

for instance, recognizing cacao and cocoa butter percent-
ages, qualities about which learned people agree, and then
choosing with that knowledge. For that matter, what *isn't*
learned? Cats who have been reared with rats do not hunt
and kill them. While hardwired emotions, bodily reactions to
threat or reward, are primal, feelings are the mind's process-
ing of a bodily state. Feelings, which are learned, vary from
person to person, and people are shaped by their cultures.
Fried crickets are a bar snack in Thailand. Ant soup is common in China.

Citing research at the Chemical Senses Center in
Philadelphia, Frank Bruni writes that our taste for food is *not*
physiological. In other words, it's not a matter of taste buds
or "a palate" but rather psychology. Taste is a "function of
expectation, emulation, adaptation." A taste for something
we may initially dislike, for instance cilantro or lamb, can be
learned. With repeated exposure, even people with "soapy
taste" receptors for cilantro can learn to love it.

If something as apparently instinctual and visceral as a
taste for food can be learned, then almost *everything* can be
learned. Albeit not easily or quickly or to the point of expertise. And only if the learner is willing. I will never learn
advanced math, but that is my choice, albeit a choice based
on lack of talent for math. Maybe talent is overrated; as Joyce
Carol Oates says, "there's only the work." I believe that most
people can learn anything, although I prefer to learn more
about things about which I have some knowledge, like literature or food.

Just as I've evolved from Hershey's to Bonnat, I've evolved
from the dry debris of supermarket tea bags to fresh tea
leaves ordered from growers or online purveyors. My favorite

THE PERFORMANCE OF TASTE

type of *Camellia sinesis* is oolong. I can distinguish between varieties and, in one case, can tell whether a milk oolong is natural or has added flavor. Natural milk oolong has a creamy flavor that does not come from milk. The Taiwanese variety is expensive, so price is one indicator. Because my first milk oolong was of excellent quality, now my taste buds notice when it's not the real thing, which is the result of terroir, the soil and climate it was grown in. Something added, exaggerated, something not quite right. How is the reality of anything determined?

Henry James's short story "The Real Thing" is narrated by a painter who employs a genteel and financially desperate married couple (the Monarchs) as models for his illustrations in potboiler novels. To their dismay, the painter eventually realizes that his previous, working-class models "do" nobility better. Of Mrs. Monarch, the painter says, "She was always a lady certainly, and into the bargain was always the same lady. She was the real thing, but always the same thing. There were moments when I was oppressed by the serenity of her confidence that she was the real thing." Mrs. Monarch's stubborn performance, her "serenity" in her own habit, prevents her from moving, figuratively as well as literally. She controls her emotions to such a degree that they cannot move others. She withholds the most vulnerable aspect of her nature. The Monarchs have lost their money, but they cling to their class superiority. James's story dates from a period when class distinctions were being shored up precisely because they were being challenged. The story suggests that class is a learnable set of behaviors, a *performance*, not an intrinsic quality. James antedates the insights of Goffman, of Foucault, of Derrida, of

Butler, by suggesting that there is no core individual self that cannot change and learn. Indeed, at the end of the story, Mrs. Monarch does change, evidenced by her serving tea to the Cockney model and doing the young woman's hair.

When it comes to the taste of food, say a tomato, the "real thing" is an extremely complex set of flavors. In *The Dorito Effect: The Surprising New Truth about Food and Flavor,* Mark Schatzker points out that because these flavors have been chemically replicated and enhanced to produce such things as tomato-flavored chips, the laboratory version often supplies only flavor, not nutrition. This leads to two things: overeating and yet undernourishment because people are not absorbing the nutrients of a real tomato. Moreover, as Jo Robinson argues in *Eating on the Wild Side,* the bland taste of agribusiness tomatoes is linked to their lack of nutrients. With food, the real thing gives life. Like a counterfeit tomato, a human being's performance is not usually lethal but might still be harmful.

Connoisseurship represents the highest level of achievement and learning. Thanks to art history classes and museum-going, I recognize the work of many painters, but I would never presume to distinguish an original from a forgery. My knowledge is superficial. Perhaps the word "connoisseur" does not have as strong a taint of pretension in the fields of wine or visual art because understanding these commodities demands so much training, relying on science as much as taste. Americans have a conflicted relationship with education, training, and expertise. In Switzerland, for example, these things are respected, to the point that people's degrees are part of the way they are addressed. In the United States, we only agree with a medical doctor's right to pronounce his degree with his name.

When the substance under consideration is accessible to everyone, however, Americans apply the label "snob" to those who perform their taste. Linguist Charlene Elliott points out that ordinary commodities like coffee have recently been made fields for connoisseurship, while previously elite commodities like wine have been democratized. Starbucks allows everyone to be a coffee connoisseur, which nudges some enthusiasts to engage in one-upmanship. Wine-tasting classes at shops and through community education give many more people the language to describe what they are tasting: wood, steel, stone, flint, berry, citrus, spritz, and so on. Robert Parker's point system, however, not only belies the complexity of wine, it assumes the favored criteria, for example an American taste for "big" and sweeter wines. Since my childhood, restaurant food in America's large cities has become as good as or better than that in large cities elsewhere, including Paris.

Is our reluctance to recognize the value of learning a form of anti-intellectualism? Is American unwillingness to accept expertise related to an idea of fairness, of hearing all sides even if one of those sides is patently wrong—for example, by including a climate-change denier on a panel of experts? Perhaps it is an American notion of democracy to insist that everyone's opinion is equal in every way and at the same time insist that "taste" is so individual it cannot be argued with.

Literature also falls into this category of democratization. In the United States, we have the sense that anybody who reads can critique, ancillary to the notion that anyone can write if they just sit down and do it. The shift from the professional reviewer to the amateur and often anonymous reader—facilitated by the cultural revolution of the internet—has been noted by many theorists. One of the earliest was Linda Hutcheon, who proposes that this shift simplified evaluation, the awarding of stars or points (like Parker's wine system) as opposed to more nuanced analysis. Whereas reviewers' opinions previously had authority because of their training and reputation, now reviews are democratized. Professional critics are no longer arbiters of taste. Amateur critic-reviewers use platforms such as Amazon, Goodreads, and Tripadvisor to establish themselves by the quantity of reviews, or sometimes merely to declaim or laud a specific thing. Hutcheon points out that consumer reviews invite further response from readers, widening the context for "response-ability," and extending aesthetics to include morals and ethics. Yet technology's role in fabricating a psychic sense of self is not yet clear: as Zadie Smith remarks in her review of the film *The Social Network*, "When a human being becomes a set of data as on a website like Facebook, he or she is reduced."

The word "snob" once meant the opposite of what it means today. In the late eighteenth century, the word referred to a shoemaker or his apprentice, then to anyone who was not a Cambridge student. Although etymological research reveals it probably does not come from *sine nobilitate*, "without nobility," the gist is the same. A snob used to be someone who was working class. By the mid-nineteenth century, the word referred to people who "imitated the habits of their social superiors." It carries the sense of sham: they hadn't come by these habits through bloodline and breeding. In other words, they hadn't learned them *at home*, like James's couple, the Monarchs. The word "snob" was coined as a response to the anxiety of not recognizing strangers, not knowing where to place them in a social schema, not knowing whom to trust. Medieval villages with a clear social hierarchy—where everyone knew everyone else—differ from cities where strangers from various places encounter one another. Historian and philosopher Michel Foucault argues that legal systems, universities, hospitals, and prisons were among the institutions developed to manage these growing populations of strangers starting in the seventeenth century.

Because of newly intersecting social classes, people were also more likely to be conned. Obviously, a confidence trick can only be successfully performed when the recipient doesn't know the con man. Thus, anxiety in determining "the real thing" increases as opportunities for being fooled multiply. Jean Baudrillard believes the difference between the real thing and the image or copy is erased in our postmodern era. The US presidential election of 2016 can be cited as an example in which "fake news" and falsehoods stood as facts. Today's connoisseur performs her taste in a world that is suspicious of learning and disinclined to trust expertise, a world that also increasingly disregards facts.

What I read affects me on as visceral a level as what I eat. I can read the first page of a book and realize that it will neither delight nor nourish me. These judgments grow out of the fact that I have spent more time with literature—reading and writing it, learning about it, teaching it—than with anything else. Literary professionals earn an education that separates them from general readers. Janice Radway sees the gulf of purpose between academics and general readers. Although both groups read to understand how to live, academics also read to explicate, to discriminate, and to judge. Academics are trained to dissect and judge literature in formal ways, and this training unites them, something made clear to me when I was asked to participate in a model book group at the Salt Lake Public Library. The leaders had put together as "diverse" a group as possible: a disabled Chicano lawyer, a Mormon woman in her seventies, a Mormon writer of adolescent fiction, a Latino professor of communication, a humor writer, a judge, a recent college graduate and poetry-slam winner originally from Tonga, the associate director of the Utah Humanities Council, and two university poets. Interestingly, those of us with graduate degrees in literature had more in common with each other than with anyone else, despite racial, ethnic, or religious differences, because we had been trained to analyze literature formally *and* contextually. Everyone else in the group responded to the "feel-good" message of Barbara Kingsolver's *The Bean Trees,* but the four literary professionals focused on form and on the disappointing simplicity of the characters. We would have liked a more complex book, one whose problems inspired debate.

Each year I attend thirty or more literary readings sponsored either by the colleges where I teach or by bookstores and community organizations. Their quality varies in both performance (writers are not necessarily good readers of their work) and in the writing itself. Literature teaches us how to live, so consequently, subjects such as race, class, gender, and sexual orientation are central to it. Sometimes I feel as Keats did when he wrote about discovering a new translation, "like some watcher of the skies / when a new planet swims into his ken." Other times, I am held hostage.

At one literary nonfiction reading a few years ago, when the writer (who is white) reached an insight about her spiritual journey that she thought brilliant (signified by the dramatic pause)—"we are all slaves"—I stifled the urge to moan. In his second annual message to Congress on December 1, 1862, Abraham Lincoln said, "In giving freedom to the slave, we assure freedom to the free." But the white writer who said "we are all slaves" was attempting to connect human beings by equating all varieties of psychological, social, and historical bondage. Apparently her insight came to her in an all-black church, a journey that caused her to leave her "comfort zone."

In a classroom, I would have asked how that essay might avoid a phrase that dumps disparate human experience into one basket. I would have asked her how, precisely, she felt "enslaved" and to distinguish that feeling from those expressed in slave narratives. My own understanding of race is neither instinctive nor comprehensive, and it continues to change. I could list many instances where my lack resulted in offense, such as the time I entered a classroom containing a white man and a black woman and I mistook the woman for the student instead of the professor. Or the time I mistook one black woman for another.

But the reading I attended was not in a classroom, and the writer's introduction included the fact that the essay had been published *and* cited as "notable" in an anthology. Of course, within the broad category of "publishable" are subjective criteria not universally agreed upon, criteria that change over time and vary by place. Shakespeare's tragedies were rewritten by Nahum Tate in the eighteenth century. Today, who reads Vachel Lindsay's much-anthologized 1919 poem "The Congo" (subtitled "A Study of the Negro Race" and beginning, "Fat black bucks in a wine-barrel room") without a roll of the eyes? Each era has a threshold for publication, and ours is low. Publishing is a democracy, I tell students, a conversation that anyone can enter, *somewhere.* The fast-and-easy publishing offered by the internet and print-on-demand can bypass gatekeepers. Anyone can edit a literary magazine or start a press, but not everyone is an editor who can, as poet William Stafford said, save a writer from embarrassment. Once an essay is published, its chance of being critiqued is slim, because our culture produces far more than it reviews. Moreover, reviews might be written by someone who hasn't thought deeply about literature, issues of identity, or much of anything else.

When I used to review books, I reviewed only those I liked. In fact, when sent books by a journal, I was told to choose ones for a positive review. I reassured myself that I was following this practice because I didn't want to waste time on bad books, but the truth is I also didn't want to risk the personal fallout of a negative review. Early in his career, a colleague used his intellect and wit to negatively review books by senior poets. Although the reviews were fair—even famous poets publish bad books—one poet didn't take the criticism well and began a vendetta against my colleague, then in his thirties. Because the world of literary art—especially the poetry world—is small, my colleague was hurt professionally.

But writing and reading solely positive reviews is often not as instructive as fuller critiques. By learning what's not good, we learn what is. Because of the fallout, negative literary reviewing is done privately, if at all, via gossip. At that reading, the teacher in me was irked—both that the writer didn't realize how bad the piece is and that an editor had chosen it for publication. I had encouraged my students to attend that reading. Looking around and seeing them there in the audience, I worried that they thought I had endorsed the work.

Alongside a plethora of venues and a paucity of critique is the assumption that creative writing is a form of expression, not a form of thought. We imagine it's unfair to criticize personal experience. Who are we to challenge what the writer *felt*? This is akin to challenging someone's taste for a specific food and is based on the assumption that feelings are not learned. That they are inviolable, like a taste (or not) for chocolate. Yet woven with feelings that *are in fact learned* is an argument that must be questioned, especially when its assumptions affect all of us. Perhaps that's the difference between my judgments about food and my judgments about literature. My not eating at a particular restaurant restricts the offense to a few friends. My silence at a piece that lumps the experience of enslaved people together with that of a privileged white woman goes beyond the personal.

The ancient Greeks and Romans routinely hissed and booed performances they did not like. Today it's rare for audiences to offer any negative reaction. At poetry slams, racism or sexism in a piece might be booed, but even then, the stage is largely a protected space, a place for praise. We come to readings to provide community for the writer, hoping for, in Horace's words, instruction or delight. Although we might get neither, we still applaud at the end.

In Quaker circles, the reading might have been treated to silent reflection, as applause inappropriately focuses on the individual's ego. In US literary circles, being nice is more important than being truthful, and silence seems rude. Or perhaps booing or withholding applause—especially when writing has been published—is just too late.

While more than a few of the readings I attend offer self-indulgent or trite work, even those writers tend to be cautious with the subjects of gender and class, not leaping to the conclusion that "we are all women" or "we are all proletarian" in an attempt to establish solidarity. By contrast, "we are all slaves" is a flashpoint. Yet for every Cliven Bundy, the Nevada rancher who recently wondered if blacks were "better off" during slavery, there are a thousand people whose misguided ideas about race receive polite applause.

When creative writers are offered only praise, including the default praise of publication, they aren't pushed to improve. By contrast, at a Toastmasters meeting, the audience gives feedback on both argument and delivery. Similarly, a scholar's argument and its assumptions would be rigorously questioned by more than one person due to the critical response built into both scholarly conference presentations and peer-reviewed publication. Beyond literature, restaurant reviews in large cities with a demanding clientele offer a chef honest—and often negative—critique.

"There is nothing permanent except change," said Heraclitus. Stoneground has a new chef. The Mainos have gone out of the chocolate business. Friendships in Laura's group have dissolved. Perhaps the writer of "we are all slaves" realizes her error, despite the fact that one of her Amazon reader reviews praises this exact insight.

As for me, eight years after that birthday celebration, I take a deep breath and look away when I see someone using the dangerous knee machine at the gym. I'm more conscious about when I perform my knowledge of food. I try not to hurt someone's feelings, but I won't eat what I don't want to eat. I'd rather not go than pretend enjoyment, and Laura understands this. On the other hand, when there's something more important than food involved, I try to be less cautious. When I published a bit of my reaction to "we are all slaves" as a blog post, one man called it "passive-aggressive." Yes. Because I didn't have the nerve to *say* something to the writer, I'm thinking through my lack of performance at that moment with the essay you are reading. I could excise my discussion of that reading and make this essay solely about food, less obviously political than literature. I could name the writer and make my disagreement public, but that would focus more on her lapse than my own.

I don't want to waste the time that I have left on earth, either by eating food I don't like or by holding my tongue in cowardice. Or by hurting people's feelings. We live in a world where genetically modified food and "fake facts" require us to judge them, and to speak when it could make a difference in someone else's life. What good is knowledge if it doesn't teach us how to live? What could be more important than doing the right thing, whatever that might be?

Taking Leave

IN TRIESTE BEFORE WORLD WAR I, WORKING AS A TUTOR, James Joyce wrote a prose poem whose subjects include his crush on one of his Jewish students. The posthumously published "Giacomo Joyce" is a reverie on beauty and mortality with the lines, "Youth has an end: the end is here. It will never be. You know that well. What then? Write it, damn you, write it! What else are you good for?"

What else are you good for? Joyce's question reveals his emotional life as the source for his art. The passage points to nostalgia—longing for lost time—as an instigating emotion. When he returned to Trieste after World War I, Joyce was saddened by its decline. The city had lost not only its importance as the second busiest port in Europe, it had become less cosmopolitan, more insular, with obvious xenophobia and anti-Semitism. Writer John McCourt makes the case that Trieste stood in for Dublin in *Ulysses*, with the same "shabby genteel" look, the "tarry tang" of the sea, and the same "bittersweet melancholy." It seems writers can turn places they've traveled to into a piece of themselves—or vice versa. Joyce never returned to Ireland to live, although he wrote, "For myself, I always write about Dublin, because if I can get to the heart of Dublin I can get to the heart of all the cities of the world. In the particular is contained the universal." Similarly, Marco Polo in Italo Calvino's novel *Invisible Cities* says, "Every time I describe a city I am saying something about Venice." Dublin was not just Joyce's motif, it was his raison d'être, but most of his encounters with it took place in his memory and in his imagination.

Notwithstanding the occasional romance between a native and a traveler, the traveler is only authorized to be "other," to observe and to participate in superficial layers of the foreign culture. She should not steal a rock from the Acropolis nor scratch a name into a tree. Yet cities are replete with *aides-mémoires*. I remember walking through a small square in Trieste and seeing a statue of Italo Svevo, the pen name for Ettore Schmitz, another Jewish student and friend of James Joyce. Joyce championed Svevo's novel *Confessions of Zeno* (or *Zeno's Conscience*), the fictional journal of a businessman undergoing psychoanalysis. The narrator's contradictory, ironic, and neurotic attitudes advertise the book's modernity: it's impossible to imagine that tone in a previous era. Bits of the novel, which I'd read in my twenties, trickled back to me when I saw the statue of the author. I imagined Zeno sneaking around this city too small to hide in. "A confession in writing is always a lie," says Zeno, an idea I did not understand so many years ago. Writing enables an author to make herself wiser or more likable.

Trieste is a city of 205,000 people tucked on a narrow strip of eastern Italian Adriatic coast, a city that is not a tourist destination—Joyce called it "docile." My cousin calls it "dull and geriatric" compared to his city of Ljubljana, Slovenia, where a fifth of the population is students. Of course, Slovenians also say "Trieste is ours," which makes perfect sense if you look at a map. The city enjoys a backdrop of majestic lime-stone mountains and a front parlor facing the sea. Mountains and sea together, I think, comprise the earth's most stunning beauty, a combination that makes us think we can have it all: the past, the present, and a future.

Maybe because it is as Austro-Hungarian as it is Italian or because it adjoins Slovenia, where I have family, or just because I've visited so often, I feel comfortable in Trieste. The Piazza Unità d'Italia is the largest square in Europe facing the sea, built when the city's fortunes were grander. With the rise of fascism after World War I, Slovenes in Trieste were expelled and their businesses destroyed. A photo taken on September 18, 1938, shows Mussolini speaking to a crowd that fills the square. He was announcing new racial laws that would re-strict Jews' civil rights, ban their books, and seize their as-sets. When I visited the city with Laura, we were touched by Trieste's changing destiny as well as its architecture.

Once, on a sunny day in the Piazza Unità d'Italia, I stood in a circle of adult writing students and one other faculty member, hoping I might break away to wander. One of the students, in his twenties, spoke up. "I don't want to trudge around here," he said. Meanwhile, my colleague took off his hat and wiped his brow.

Trudge? My mouth must have hung open, but I didn't protest the group decision to leave. After three hours, how did the student know he was done with Trieste? Maybe he was just tired, but I wonder if our first stop that morning, the haunted space of Risiera di San Sabba, the rice mill turned into the only concentration camp in Italy, had made him in-capable of enjoying the architecture of the square. Indeed, having been to the Risiera previously, I had not wanted to visit again, so while my group toured the spectral grounds, I wandered the aisles of a discount store around the corner.

In the vast and nearly empty piazza with its view of the sea—as I think of it now—my brain has room to escape its cramped attic. I feel a little relieved of my neuroses there. Perhaps I also enjoy Trieste because I'm not one of thirty thousand tourists, as in Venice. It's a human longing to not feel like one of many. We like to be recognized when we are traveling, to be the most favored or the ones with inside information, information that makes us feel that we are not in fact tourists. Cities are sources of bourgeois pleasures, but they should also dislodge a preconception or instill a new idea. We take home—along with the sea salt and bay leaves— a shift in thinking, a new intelligence. The Nazi operation at Risiera marked both its Austro-Hungarian past and its geographical centrality, and after the war the camp served as a transit center for refugees fleeing Communist Yugoslavia. My father was probably processed there—I wish I had thought to ask him before he died.

"Memory's images," says Marco Polo in *Invisible Cities*, "once they are fixed in words, are erased." Indeed, research shows that once we take a photograph of something, we do not remember it as well, almost as if the camera and photo take over the work of remembering. We relax our hold on the image. In writing, I might be erasing stored images to make room for new ones. I am certainly sharing them, giving the memories a collective potential, akin to the way reading has enlarged my own storehouse. The brain is a "mechanism for collecting memories of the past in order to use them continually to predict the future," Carlo Rovelli writes. Our human future looks grim. Fascism is once again on the rise. Misinformation about the Holocaust is increasing, as survivors die and the events seem distant. According to a 2019 study commissioned by the Conference on Jewish Material Claims against Germany, most Americans "believe something like the Holocaust could happen again," but 41 percent of millennials do not know that in the Holocaust six million Jews were killed, along with eleven million other people whom Fascists deemed unworthy: Communists and other political adversaries, Roma, Catholics, Muslims, Slavs, people of color, mentally or physically disabled people, LGBT folk, and others. Who can read the news today and not worry about the future?

Laura is 5′9″, an Irish strawberry-blonde with an easy athleticism. I am 5′4″ and a brown-going-gray mittel-European. Nonetheless, strangers sometimes ask, "Are you sisters?" Maybe people see the love between Laura and me, the closeness, and have no other frame for it. Straight women friends get asked this, too, as if there can be no nonblood bonds between women. We know another lesbian couple who, when asked this question, simply answer, "Yes." We laugh, understanding that they are deflecting the homophobia or prurient curiosity behind the question. "We're here, we're queer, get used to it" makes a positive issue of sexual orientation. Sisters are a neutral beige. A lesbian couple can require an opinion, and in a monogamous society, a woman attracted to both men and women cannot simultaneously perform both attractions. One attraction is always suspect. The performance of gender also raises questions. My "German femme style"—no makeup, short hair, sensible but I hope attractive clothes—allows me to blend in most of the time. Of course, the older I get, the less I am seen as a sexual being, which has advantages allied to those of bisexuality. I can pass for being beyond sex. In the Seattle Museum of Art on our first trip together, I realized that my attraction to Laura could be consummated in a public restroom. She laughed, "I wondered when you would figure that out."

Traveling women have always had to think about how men will react. Like rabbits sniffing for predators, we look for the safe place to sleep. Once, in my twenties on a Greek ferry, when what was supposed to have been a day trip turned into an overnight because of bad weather, I didn't want to sleep on deck. Most of the crew had left the ship for a night on the town, including the purser, so I claimed an empty cabin in a deserted corridor and placed my backpack against the unlockable door. A crew member found me. I tried to explain I would pay in the morning. He returned with a bottle of lemon soda. It struck me that the next man who tried my door might not be so civil, so I returned to the windy deck.

Another time, on a night train, stretched out on an entire side of a six-person compartment, I awoke with a sour rush of fear to the sight of a young man opposite me. He reached for the purse at my feet. I froze. Lifting it, he motioned for me to raise my head, which I did. He placed my purse under my head, nodded, and left. I know I was lucky, and those instances taught me caution as much as they instilled gratitude. While my years of solo budget travel ingrained resilience alongside exhilarating freedom, travel with Laura in late middle age is a comfortable pleasure. We are stronger together. Sometimes when I take her hand or sense her warmth beside me, I marvel at my good fortune.

In Split, Laura and I recognized and were recognized by our gay waiter. Homosexuality is no longer forbidden by law in Croatia, but it's still not a place where we should kiss in public. Travel guides say homosexuality is "tolerated," no doubt more in tourists than in natives. Tourists, a source of income, don't integrate into the culture and they can't change it. Our waiter brought us a carafe of tap water instead of trying to sell us bottled. "Our tap water is excellent," he said with a smile, "but don't tell anyone I brought you this." A good waiter makes guests feel at home. In fact, we did return to the restaurant. We liked the food—and him.

About Venice, more than a hundred years ago, Henry James noted, "there is nothing left to discover or describe and originality of attitude is completely impossible." What *is* always left to discover is one's emotional state. I remember now that Sunday morning when Laura and I were heading for Marco Polo International Airport. We needed to fill the car with gas but drove farther and farther away from the airport while trying to find an open station that would either take credit cards or a hundred-euro note. "This is nuts," Laura said after a frustrating hour and a half. "Let's return the car empty and pay the penalty." I reluctantly agreed. Then we discovered an open gas station right next to the rental car return. Our American habits—car rentals make it hard to be frugal—told us it couldn't possibly be that simple. My penny-pinching added a layer of anxiety. I don't regret that irritation with each other and our paper map and my broken Italian. The morning was anchored by fear of missing a plane and anxiety about running empty.

That morning I realized that the willingness to spend money—to waste it, even—is an insurance policy. It was something I had to relearn. We reached the point where our anger was directed more at each other than the situation. And then relief—and laughter—cleansed that anger like rain upon a dusty windshield. Indeed, humans remember what is linked to emotions, mostly bad: the humiliation of a menstrual accident on a white silk-covered chair, the terror of ripping open a knee on an outcropping of rock, the frustration of a silly argument with a traveling companion over the nature of semolina.

One of my bad habits is offering people information they may not want. Another is the sense that I must control everything and everyone around me, that everything's my responsibility and if I slack off, who knows what will happen? This habit is impossible to maintain while traveling, which makes me a predictable and often irritating companion. I figure out where we stay and eat and what we see, but I also frustrate my companions by assuming they feel as I do. On one flight home, I said, "Next time, let's see Corsica," but the best friend sitting next to me was secretly swearing, "Never again." She told me this years later when she had already broken her vow never again to travel with me. Laura accepts our bargain, rebelling only rarely, because her desire to please is as strong as my desire to control. And perhaps because our travel is always my idea.

"I have no reason to go, except that I have never been, and knowledge is better than ignorance. What better reason could there be for traveling?" said Freya Stark, a British explorer and writer who settled in the small town of Asolo, north of Venice. But she also returned to places where she had traveled, becoming an expert on the Middle East. Novelty and stimulation, distraction and avoidance, education and relaxation, pleasure or pain: there are as many reasons to travel as reasons to do anything. It isn't always necessary to know one's reasons. I'm reminded of my effort to learn to draw a few years ago. My teacher asked me to draw the head of the model, and I drew an oval. "You've limited yourself from the start," he said. "What if you started from the inside and worked your way out?" When I tried it that way, my strokes were tentative, delicate. I shaded ovals for eyes, darkening the pupils. Then I realized the eyes needed glints of reflected light that would require me to erase some of the dark. Seeing does require beginning from the inside, discovering how and why one thinks, and travel constantly demands that we see.

When in Venice on that Adriatic trip, Laura and I did not stay near the train station. It seems stupid to have done that in the past, just to save the cost of a vaporetto ride. We stayed on Giudecca, which has three luxury hotels, a few cheaper ones, one monastery, and plenty of Venetians. We caught glimpses of nontourist life in this watery place, almost everything laboriously brought in by boat. A man fishing from steps and a cat waiting for the catch. Schoolchildren with backpacks. Giudecca is one place in Venice where, due to the size and layout of the island with its view of San Marco, I cannot get lost. While getting lost can be a glorious part of travel, it's also nice to find one's bed.

Giudecca, shaped like a fat segmented worm, is formed from spits of land connected by concrete bridges. It hosts gardens and two Palladio churches. One is Il Redentore, built to thank God for deliverance from a plague outbreak during which a quarter of the city's inhabitants died. The many steps to the entrance are designed to increase the pilgrim's devotion. Revisiting a city creates steps that increase devotion, and not only for one's investment of valuable time. Knowing a place strengthens my hold on it—I believe I have a right to recommend or denounce it, a satisfying step toward expertise.

Coming and going, we passed a lovely restaurant named I Figli delle Stelle. Figs in the stars, I thought, before I realized it's children of the stars, that song playing everywhere the first time I was in Venice in 1977. Alan Sorrenti's falsetto, pop and disco, and a guitar riff that makes you want to dance. Like most pop songs, it has silly lyrics: "We are children of the stars / without history / ageless / heroes of a dream." It's not possible, much less desirable, to be without history. While hardwired human emotions don't change, structures change, as do feelings, as do the way humans think about our lives, and if we don't keep track of these changes, we are doomed to swimming in circles in a fishbowl in a dark closet.

Laura and I didn't eat at I Figli delle Stelle because we did not make it a priority, allowing weariness or convenience to take precedence, like being carried by waves to the shore. Mussels and clams. Orecchiette, little ears, nubs of pasta. Watermelon sorbetto. A bottle of Foss Marai prosecco. What did I miss? Reading the menu is not enough to satisfy my curiosity, my desire for pleasure. Maybe someday I will eat at I Figli delle Stelle, I tell myself. If it stays in business. If I go back to Venice. If I'm not "done" with that city. Perhaps a winter visit, empty *campi*, and a fine drizzle of rain. This image makes me want to get on a plane right now.

Maybe my inability to admit I'm done with Venice—or, for that matter, Trieste—is nostalgia. Writer Svetlana Boym

argues that nostalgia is a "symptom of our age, an historical emotion." She writes: "The nostalgic desires to obliterate
history and turn it into private or collective mythology, to
revisit time as space, refusing to surrender to the irreversibility of time that plagues the human condition." The desire to
make history into mythology is always a risk in writing about
one's own life, perhaps more generally in writing, period.
Writers can escape that trap by theorizing their recounting
of events—by asking why they are telling one thing and not
another. But the answers are not always clear.

Perhaps I am nostalgic for my childhood Europe, the place
I remember only in scattered images and feelings. No place
remains for our return. The not-belonging to any place drives
me to question wherever I am, and to wonder if there might
exist a place where I do not chafe against norms, where I am
content. Instead of always searching for context, for motive,
for depth, perhaps I could float unanchored. Like a jellyfish.
Unlikely, but perhaps.

Sometimes, when boarding a plane to leave a place, I feel a
rush of fondness, coveting what I had just experienced there,
even if what I had experienced was not interesting or beautiful. I deny the irreversibility of time by promising myself that
I can come back. Perhaps revisiting time as space is to visit
time out of time—that is what it feels like to enter the space
of Zvonimir Mihanović's paintings. Experiencing art, we are
in a moving train watching a stationary train, a dizzying state.

Rereading a book can be like returning to the doorframe
where our parents have penciled in our height: we learn that
we have changed. As Aristotle said, "Time is nothing other
than the measure of change." The first time I read Henry
James's *The Golden Bowl*, I was working in an office in Paris,

making coffee and answering the phone for a man who needed someone to run interference between his girlfriends and his wife. In my ninety-square-foot sixth-floor walkup maid's room, I identified with Charlotte because she had no money, no career, no family. Unmoored, she traveled to find a reason to stay.

Years later, married, I reread the book, and my sympathies moved to Maggie. She gave up her father to keep her husband. I had begun to see cracks in the golden bowls of this life, the cost of fidelity. The third time I read the book, in graduate school, I read it even more closely, feeling the convoluted prose reflect the convoluted natures of friendship and marriage. *Maggie came on with her heart in her hands; she came on with the definite prevision, throbbing like the tick of a watch, of a doom impossibly sharp and hard, but to which, after looking at it with her eyes wide open, she had none the less bowed her head.*

To look at doom with one's eyes wide open and then bow one's head to it: a definition of maturity. The novel was as good as I had remembered; I just found different things to admire. Upon rereading E. M. Forster's *Howard's End*, Vivian Gornick found herself "dismayed not only by how much I had got wrong but how much in the book is wrong—the sexual naïveté, the rhetorical posturing, the hand from the grave all read like hokum today." After reading *The Golden Bowl* for the third time, I concluded that James found a prose style to make vivid betrayal, integrity, and the transactional nature of relationships, but I won't return to *The Golden Bowl*; there are too many other books to read.

Unlike rereading books, which costs only time, travel is a luxury that also costs money. Sometimes wasting it. That makes it an ultimate luxury. This is something I learn from Laura—not only the willingness to pay a penalty for an empty gas tank in exchange for peace of mind, but also to take the long view. When I was twenty-one, I saw Rudolf Nureyev dance in Paris in an obstructed-view seat because I was trying to save money. The man I was with said, "I'd rather sit in hundred-franc seats for half my life, than fifty-franc seats for a whole life." He had grown up more financially secure than I. Now that I earn more than seventy-five dollars a week, I agree. But it's taken me forty years to get here.

When I tell Laura that during each of the two years I worked in Europe after college I took three months to travel, she asks, "What gave you the idea?" In Laura's family, travel, especially overseas, was considered frivolous and dangerous. Neither parent had been out of the United States, and Laura's first trip abroad was our semester-long stay in the south of France, where I had a fellowship and when she was able to quit her job to accompany me. For a moment I felt proud of my gumption. But in truth, for me to travel back to Europe in my early twenties was in some ways more comfortable than living in the United States with its demands of assimilation. Traveling gave me the luxury of time out, without rent or possessions or deadlines. Working in Europe made me learn a region's terroir by filtering my emotional life through exchanges with coworkers, through climate and weather and landscape. There's a reason small talk centers on the weather: it affects every aspect of human life, especially our moods.

While traveling alone, my feelings are internal, encapsulated in my body as it moves through places. I never kept a journal. I'd like to relive those years with my mature mind, improving them as if they were a rough draft. Perhaps I have done that with this book. It's doubly a privilege to be able to travel when young—with a strong body and an infinite sense of time—but travel might also be wasted on the young. Not entirely, though.

In that period of European work and travel after college, I came to understand as opposite sides of the same coin my fundamental loneliness and my self-sufficiency. I also discovered that I missed the United States and its brash possibilities, American ingenuity and risk, our value of individual, rather than communal, measures of behavior. When German pedestrians held out their arms to stop me from crossing against the light, how dare they prevent me from being run over by a bus!

Luigi Barzini begins *The Italians* with a chapter on the tourist invasion, asking why Italy is so popular. His answer: Italy not only has everything a traveler desires—history, landscape, culture—but a variety of it. British journalist John Hooper updates Barzini: "No people on earth express themselves as visually as the Italians." Neurologically, the visual sense is the most sophisticated, what we revel in as we travel, and afterward, through postcards and photographs and essays. Whether the image is the roiling briny-green sea in front of us, a photograph of it, or just a description, our brains are stimulated.

It must be the more primitive senses of smell, touch, and taste that make us want—I first wrote "hunger for"—the physicality of travel. Imagination spurred by reading is not enough, despite the Chinese saying about traveling while reading in an armchair. I wish I had a plate of *Amanita caesarea* right now, and looking at pictures of the red-capped mushroom and imagining its vegetal, otherworldly taste isn't good enough. In his *Duino Elegies*, Rainer Maria Rilke mentions "the great initial letter of Thereness"—the first excitement and simultaneity of being in a place and an emotional state. I wish I could stroll along the sea path next to Duino Castle, not because I want to feel close to Rilke's genius, but because I want to notice, again for the first time, the laurel bushes, fragrant leaves free for the picking. (And smuggle a bag back home to let those leaves flavor my soups.)

Would I go back? What would it cost? I never tire of the game, "How much would you have to be paid in order to..." Row back to the island after just having rowed *to and from* the island? Sleep on the deck of the ferry? Jump into a canal? Both Laura and I would jump into a murky canal for one thousand dollars. Less than half the cost of one night at the Hotel Cipriani. At twenty-two when I couldn't sleep in the no-star *pensione* for the mosquitoes whirring in through the open windows and around my ears, I would have jumped in for a whole lot less. Baudrillard would call this an example of exchange value in late capitalism. I've never been given an actual dare upon which I could earn money, although thinking about potential challenges provides different compensation. It forces me to assign value and to assess, to realize that everything I do and don't do has meaning.

I want to go to Asia, to South America, to Australia and New Zealand, but not enough to plan a trip and spend the money. At least not yet. I want to go to Cuba but not enough to spend five thousand dollars. Not yet. I envy a friend whose son lived in China and later traveled with his American parents, using his fluent Mandarin and other cultural familiarity to give them glimpses of nontourist life. I'd like to go to Africa but I need a spur, like a friend who lives there. Having friends in Israel and Jordan allowed me to visit those countries some years ago. I want, I want.

Media blur the line between needs and desires. I have the pastime of shopping on the internet for hotels, even for places I have no plans to visit. I fantasize, get off cheaply. I relish closely reading travelers' reviews, reading between the lines, looking at the "gallery" of photos and imagine slipping the front desk clerk twenty dollars for a better room, choosing fruit and local cheese for breakfast in the sun-filled dining room. I also look at the websites of hotels *after* I have stayed there, a postmortem, juxtaposing the artful shots with my reality. The harbor is littered. The hotel pool is shallow, crowded with noisy children. The room is small and faces a brick wall.

In Trieste at the Excelsior Savoia in 2011, Laura and I were upgraded to a huge corner room with a balcony and view of the harbor. For once, the fantasy was real—and in my favorite Siamese cat colors. The hotel made me feel sleek, although we were too tired to have sex on the silk-covered king-sized bed in the sky-blue, beige, and walnut-brown room. Part of my pleasure was introducing Laura to Trieste. Through her delight, I experienced it anew. Because she loves antiquities, we spent time at the Roman ruins. We saw the synagogue, which I had never seen before. Perhaps Trieste gets an upgrade in my memory because we had a beautiful place to stay. Thinking about that room and Laura's pleasure: *nostalgia*, a memory I want to replay.

Most hotel rooms, of course, including the one in the Savoia, could be anywhere. There's no terroir, no whiff of country or culture. Seth Kugel, a former *New York Times* "Frugal Traveler," says, "Each additional dollar you spend puts up barriers between you and the world." Those months of frugal travel in my twenties opened me up to more than the pleasure of deciding my own agenda.

I live in Salt Lake City, which even on Saturday night is empty of pedestrians and their energy. At street level, the five-star Grand America hotel sports an Alcatraz-like concrete façade on three sides, no doors, sandblasted windows, a trope for the hotel's closed-off position in the city. They don't want people strolling in. During the six minutes it takes to walk a long Salt Lake block, cars whiz by and dust stirs. I point this out to a visitor and she says, "like most American cities." She's right. San Francisco is the exception, Salt Lake City the rule.

When I'm on vacation, I yearn for places different from home, home being my very own polluted, docile desert city. I yearn to be diverted, to see with new eyes, to register what I am seeing because I am not seeing it every day. Driving or even walking the same streets each day causes us to fall into a mild trance. Miles go by and I couldn't say what I saw because I wasn't really looking; I was focused on the past or the future, the irritation of the day or the plan for a weekend dinner. In the deep trance of hypnosis, the state of being lost "inside" with the id makes you incapable of critiquing the "outside." Moments feel outside of time because we access the unconscious, which is not time-bound. Sometimes, staying in one place is like being lost in the id. I need to be outside to critique the inside, to see where I am, and sometimes that outside is the past.

William Blake's tiny book of engravings, *For Children: The Gates of Paradise,* contains images worth revisiting. The best-known shows a ladder to the moon and a figure starting to climb it, with the caption "I want, I want." The figure is watched by a couple holding each other, as in awe or fear. Another, "Aged Ignorance," shows a figure with a white beard cutting the wings off a child. Blake is famous for telling us to remain childlike, with all the greed, curiosity, and intense emotion that childhood entails. And yet, without a sense of mortality, children have no understanding of the finiteness of time.

In 2015 Laura and I traveled to Europe with my then eighty-six-year-old mother and her eighty-eight-year-old sister, to visit people they loved. Laura surprised them by creating clever "Klima Sisters Alpine Tour" T-shirts, with photos of the sisters as children on front and back, and with a mountain logo, plus the dates and places of our tour. When Laura wore that shirt in a Salt Lake bakery, a woman said to her, "Where did you see them? I've heard their music."

Having Laura and her patient good humor and quick joy made the trip bearable for me, and no doubt improved it for my mother and my aunt. When I'm too bossy, Laura says with a smile, "Hey, Miss, you are not the queen of us." When I refuse to see my mother's mental decline, Laura reminds me, "Be here now." And with my confident opinions and past experiences, I am able to assuage Laura's anxieties about the safety of travel.

Near the end of our travels, on what should have been a three-hour drive from Ljubljana to Munich, we were caught up in seven hours of stalled highway misery. After all the stop-and-go clutch action, my left knee became inflamed, and with the lost time went plans for a relaxing dinner and dip in the airport hotel pool. At the apex of our frazzled tempers, my aunt (the same woman who argued for staying in a youth hostel, which I vetoed) took out the harmonica that she always carries. For half an hour of that otherwise miserable drive, she played folk songs as my mother sang along, not quite remembering words but humming on key. Two old ladies and one middle-aged one transporting themselves from the stuffy car into another realm, and another middle-aged woman learning how.

At the border between Austria and Germany, two police officers peered into our car with flashlights. Satisfied we were not illegal refugees, they let us pass. What I remember about the drive is not only the misery but how the music moved us from frustration to the primal pleasure of the moment. It will likely be the sisters' last trip to Europe.

> Who's turned us round like this, so that we always,
> do what we may, retain the attitude
> of someone who's departing? Just as he,
> on the last hill that shows him all his valley
> for the last time, will stop and linger,
> we live our lives, forever taking leave.

Thus Rilke ends his eighth Duino elegy. Sometimes we escape that attitude of departing and can substitute an attitude of joy, a willingness to be subsumed. And sometimes, instead of looking down on the valley, we look up to the stars.

Acknowledgments and Credits

This book began ten years ago, when I began writing a memoir with recipes. After a few years, I realized that I was not a writer who could combine racism with rice pilaf. I saw also that I needed help understanding the intersectionality of identity issues. Friends and colleagues rescued me. I could not have finished the book without their insights, nor without the vision and intelligence of my editor, Marguerite Avery, and the peer reviewers to whom Trinity University Press sent the manuscript. Westminster College granted me a merit leave that greatly facilitated the book's completion, and a residency at the Hermitage Artist Retreat made revising a crucial chapter a pleasure.

I am deeply grateful to the people who lit my path by reading my writing or discussing issues with me: Ranjan Adiga, Linda Aldrich, Rebecca Batt, Robin Becker, Nick Benson, Lisa Bickmore, Jean Cheney, Ben Cleary, Dawn Denham, Sean Desilets, Ellen Feld, Miles Fuller, Patricia Occhiuzzo Giggans, Bonni Goldberg, Curtis Grow, Susan Gunter, Mark Halliday, Rachel M. Hansen, Laura Inscoe, Kimberly Johnson, Linda Kauffman, Ashley Seitz Kramer, Jacqueline Lapidus, Lance Larsen, Rick Laskowski, Diane Lefer, Ann Loux, Laura Ann Manning, Madeleine Mysko, Jeff Nichols, Giancarlo Panagia, Ron Priddis, Paisley Rekdal, David Rose, Mary Ruefle, Susan

Sample, Jim Schley, John Scott, Bob Sheavly, Marc Sheehan, Barbara Strasko, Elaine Terranova, Trudy Todd, Jennifer Tonge, Holly Welker, and Janine Wittwer. Andrea Hollander discovered the title. Laurie Alberts, Camille Dungy, and Lisa Katz asked the tough questions I needed to hear: thank you especially.

Six hundred words of "The Performance of Taste" were published as a blog post for the *Chronicle of Higher Education,* and a version of the essay appeared online in the *North American Review* (2018). "Guilt: A Love Story" appeared in *Dogwood: A Journal of Poetry and Prose* (Fall 2017), and a version of "Mordwand" was published in the *Missouri Review* (Summer 2018). My thanks to the editors of these publications, especially Evelyn Somers Rogers.

NATASHA SAJÉ is the author of three award-winning poetry collections, most recently *Vivarium*, and the postmodern poetry handbook *Windows and Doors: A Poet Reads Literary Theory*. She is a professor of English at Westminster College and a faculty member in the Vermont College of Fine Arts MFA in Writing Program. She lives in Salt Lake City.